Mastering Sketch

Mastering Computer Science
Series Editor: Sufyan bin Uzayr

Mastering Sketch: A Beginner's Guide
Mathew Rooney and Md Javed Khan

Mastering C#: A Beginner's Guide
Mohamed Musthafa MC, Divya Sachdeva, and Reza Nafim

Mastering GitHub Pages: A Beginner's Guide
Sumanna Kaul and Shahryar Raz

Mastering Unity: A Beginner's Guide
Divya Sachdeva and Aruqqa Khateib

Mastering Unreal Engine: A Beginner's Guide
Divya Sachdeva and Aruqqa Khateib

Mastering Java: A Beginner's Guide
Divya Sachdeva and Natalya Ustukpayeva

For more information about this series, please visit: https://www.routledge.com/Mastering-Computer-Science/book-series/MCS

The "Mastering Computer Science" series of books are authored by the Zeba Academy team members, led by Sufyan bin Uzayr.

Zeba Academy is an EdTech venture that develops courses and content for learners primarily in STEM fields, and offers education consulting to Universities and Institutions worldwide. For more info, please visit https://zeba.academy

Mastering Sketch

A Beginner's Guide

Edited by Sufyan bin Uzayr

CRC Press
Taylor & Francis Group
Boca Raton London New York

CRC Press is an imprint of the
Taylor & Francis Group, an **informa** business

First edition published 2022
by CRC Press
6000 Broken Sound Parkway NW, Suite 300, Boca Raton, FL 33487-2742

and by CRC Press
2 Park Square, Milton Park, Abingdon, Oxon, OX14 4RN

CRC Press is an imprint of Taylor & Francis Group, LLC

ISBN: 9781032199528 (hbk)
ISBN: 9781032199504 (pbk)
ISBN: 9781003261575 (ebk)

DOI: 10.1201/9781003261575

Typeset in Minion
by KnowledgeWorks Global Ltd.

Contents

About the Editor

Sufyan bin Uzayr is a writer, coder, and entrepreneur with more than a decade of experience in the industry. He has authored several books in the past, pertaining to a diverse range of topics, ranging from History to Computers/IT.

Sufyan is the Director of Parakozm, a multinational IT company specializing in EdTech solutions. He also runs Zeba Academy, an online learning and teaching vertical with a focus on STEM fields.

Sufyan specializes in a wide variety of technologies, such as JavaScript, Dart, WordPress, Drupal, Linux, and Python. He holds multiple degrees, including ones in Management, IT, Literature, and Political Science.

Sufyan is a digital nomad, dividing his time between four countries. He has lived and taught in universities and educational institutions around the globe. Sufyan takes a keen interest in technology, politics, literature, history and sports, and in his spare time, he enjoys teaching coding and English to young students.

Learn more at sufyanism.com.

CHAPTER 1

Introduction to Sketch App

IN THIS CHAPTER

➤ To Acquire Fundamental Knowledge of Sketch and Understand Its Scope

➤ Getting Familiar with Brief History of Sketch

➤ Understanding Major Features of Sketch

➤ Learning Benefits of Sketch

➤ Installation and Setup of Sketch

Sketch is a Vector Graphic Editing software used to design the UI and UX of mobile apps and the web. In this chapter, we will be learning about the basics and concepts of Sketch. We will see a brief history of Sketch. We will also

DOI: 10.1201/9781003261575-1

see some of its significant features and benefits. We will learn about the installation and setup process. We will also see its application in a design workflow. At the end of this chapter, you will have a rough idea about Sketch, its feature, and uses.

WHAT IS SKETCH?

Sketch is a powerful, lightweight professional design application that barely takes 67 MB of storage in the disk compared to the traditional old versions of design apps or photoshops. Photoshops can take the hold up to 2 GB on the disk and is also considered slow. Once users get used to Sketch app, then they would appreciate its effectiveness over the photoshops. Bugs occur in Sketch occasionally and not too often, so considering this app for web development and beyond is appreciable. It is also cost-effective compared to other design tools such as photoshop. Working with features like Vector tools is easy. It is extensively used in Android, iOS, and web design. An infinite canvas appears on the screen as soon as you open the app. There is a toolbar, navigator, and Inspector similar to other Mac apps, and using them is pretty simple.

The scalability of vector tools is very high. It can adapt to changing styles, layouts, and sizes. Sketch supports fine-tuning. The layer list contains all the shapes we create. Complex shapes are created by combining the paths using flexible Boolean operations. From taking editability perspective, all parts can be 100% edited in Sketch. Figures are rounded to the nearest pixels' edge. Using the pixel zoom feature, one can inspect the pixels. Using the Inspector, one can control positioning, dimensions, blending modes, and opacity in Sketch. Following are the noticeable features in Sketch.

1. **Dynamic Properties:** Useful in editing position, rotation, and size of more than one object at a time. It also uses fly to perform the math operations.

2. **Layer Styles:** One can name a layer style by combining border, fills, and shadows. All of them change if any of them are altered. Users can use this on multiple objects.

3. **Multiple fills, border, and shadows:** One can use different blending modes for having unlimited solid and gradient fills.

4. **Dynamic Blur:** There are four different vibrant blurs available; Gaussian, Motion, zoom, and background.

5. **Make Exportable:** Layers can be exported directly out of Sketch.

Sketch is a vector design tool that works on the mathematical principle of Vector, whereas photoshop works on pixels. It comes between photoshop and illustrator. It allows you to add raster graphics. Sharing styles and working with the text becomes relatively easy. It enables you to work as a web designer. Users can save shared types after working on fills and styles for the object.

Canvas in photoshop is made of pixels, and objects on that canvas fall into those pixels. A Sketch is a vector tool that does not get affected by pixels. When you zoom in on the Sketch app, the edges obtained are crisp and not blur because canvas on Sketch is not made up of pixels but is made of Vector, while in photoshop, it becomes a blur as they are made up of pixels.

Vector is based on maths, and when you zoom in on the shapes, you get the line moving throughout the figures. Moving the lines, one can change the shape of the object. Sketch lets us convey ideas, visualize user flow, and demonstrate functionality.

A BRIEF HISTORY OF SKETCH

Sketch is a vector graphics editor. It was developed by a Dutch company named Sketch BV in 2010 and released on September 7, 2010. It was founded by Emanuel Sa and Pieter Omvlee. It is developed for macOS. In 2012, it won Apple Design Award. Users can use Sketch web applications on any computer. The initial idea behind releasing the first version of Sketch 1.0 was to create a lightweight, purely vector-based drawing application. Its interface is minimalistic, which hides powerful features such as rulers, grids, and powerful guides. Sketch has some incredible features, such as an infinitely large workspace, and you don't need to define the document size at starting stage. Other features include symbols, multiple pages, and easy to use slice tool.

In version 3.0, which was released on April 14, 2014, we had got the following features:

- The typical color appears in the Inspector for quick access.

- Before the previous version, where we got only four fills, this version got unlimited fillings.

- Noise is now a separate fill with variable intensity, and you also get blending options.

- The new bitmap editing tools have got the tools for cropping, selection, filling, and vectorizing.

- A simplified vector editing.

- It supports an essential text list, numbered list, and bulleted list.

- Smart resizing and scaling on Sketch Mirror and other features include more reliable networking.

- Hides all the UI during the full-screen presentation.

- Significant improvement on SVG, PDF importing.

- Got more useful web design templates.

In version 3.0.1, the developer ensured that Artboard presets and QuickLook Previews didn't get missing, and they shall appear. In version 3.0.2, performance improvement and speed were the main focus. In version 3.0.3, we got Redesigned Scripting Window with output logging for easier debugging. In version 3.0.4, the developer got updated CocoaScript.

In version 3.1, the app introduced the following new features:

- Single File as the new file format, which made it easier for the user to share.

- A toolbar button is more versatile.

- Smarter snapping.

- Redesigned pages panel for speed and convenience.

In version 3.2: speed improvement and three times support for the mirror

In version 3.2.1: PDF improvements

In version 3.2.3: reduced memory usage for complex documents

In version 3.3: connect Sketch Mirror by IP address directly, documents presets, live scale previews, and outlining shape's border had significantly better result.

In version 3.4, the following improvements happened.

- Local documents sharing.

- Improved copy and paste.

- Improved Boolean operations.

- Navigating documents becomes smoother.

In version 3.4.4: improved Sketch tool and deployment

In version 3.5: speed improvements and performance updates, especially while working for large documents and images.

In version 3.6, the following modifications are available.

- **Text improvements:** height issues.

- Better SVG support.

- Better handling of large and complex documents.

- Improved rendering.

In version 3.7, the following enhancements are available.

- Nesting symbols, setting images, and text overriding possible.

- Manual style sync.

- Missing fonts preserved.

Version 3.8: new Sketch Mirror for iOS with USB connectivity, better undo, background blur, scrolling, and catching.

In version 39, the following updates are available.

- Developer can resize symbols and groups.

- Sketch Cloud.

- New image fill type.

- Performance updates.

In version 40, the following updates are available.

- Multiple vector editing.
- Nondestructive text transformation.
- Performance and bugs fixing improved.

In version 41, the following updates are available.

- Override nested symbols with other symbols.
- Private sharing.
- WebP format export and import of images.
- Presentation mode with full screen.
- Fresh new look.

In version 42, following updates are available.

- Export presets.
- Touch bar support.

In version 43, the following updates are available.

- **Vector Editing:** Additional handles which are related to the present section are visible.

In version 44, the following updates are available.

- **Artboards:** a new section in Inspector to instruct Artboard to adjust the content size when resized.

- Rounded corners on the vector path.

- Replace missing fonts.

In version 45, the following updates are available.

- Presentation mode hides UI.

- Automatic update of plugins and disable unused plugins.

- Snap new point to exiting point.

- Color popover scrollable.

In version 46, one gets the following updates.

- Private Sharing via Sketch Cloud.

- Vertical alignment of text.

- Searchable help topics.

In version 47, the following updates are available.

- **Libraries introduced:** sharing symbols between documents possible now.

- Rectangle Corners adjustable.

In version 48, one gets the following improvements.

- sRGB and P3 color spaces available.

- Find and replace color throughout the documents.

- User can download copies from Cloud Sketch.

- Scaling of Symbol instances using the Scale command.

In version 49, the following improvements are available.

- Connecting Artboards with Links and Hotspots to create prototypes.

- Files from Cloud can be installed as libraries.

- Apple iOS 11 UI kit is now a built-in feature.

In version 50, the following updates are available.

- Better Vector Export/Import.

- Editing complex documents is more responsive and faster now.

In version 51, the following updates are available.

- Layer Styles and Text Styles are available in all documents.

- Users can now include headers and footers in prototypes.

- Improved appearance of arrows and other markers on the path.

- Many overrides.

In version 51.1, the following improvement is available.

- Sort of many more minor issues, restoration of magic wand tool, plus arrows, and other markers remain solid when applied to dashed paths.

In version 52, the following significant improvements are available.

- Improvement in UI, improved readability across the documents.

- More responsive with complex documents.

- Dark mode for macOS Mojave.

- Multiple application of Boolean operation with text layers, symbols, and shapes with outlines.

- Link layers to data sources.

- Overriding text styles and layer styles inside symbols.

In version 53, the following updates are available.

- Performance improvement for complex documents.

- New fill popover.

- Managing overriding properties directly in symbol's master.

- Overrides in symbols can be selected through a layer list.

- Improvement in snapping while moving or resizing layers.

In version 53.2, the following feature is available.

- Using new option, one can sync libraries components in a document.

In version 54, the following features are available.

- Toggling between light mode and dark mode.
- Customizable guide colors.

In version 55, the following improvements are available.

- Working with multiple layers using Smart Distribute.
- Evenly spacing becomes a simple process.
- Smart distribute works in one direction at a time.
- SVG code can generate new layers.

In version 56, the following enhancements are available.

- Text overrides in canvas are editable.
- Upgradation of Smart Distribute feature.
- Adjusting vertical and horizontal spacing between a row of layers.
- Document saving in the Sketch Cloud.

In version 56.1, the following features are available.

- Restoration of macOS AutoSave.
- Fixing crash.

In version 57, the following features are available.

- Efficient reordering of layers using smart distribution selection.

- Improvement in Boolean operations.

In version 58, one gets the following enhancement.

- **Smart layout feature:** Symbols become more power-ful and enhancing workflow when we are going to use them in our design workflow.

- Using the smart layout feature, one can set the direction for a symbol to resize.

- Different smart layout settings for nested symbols.

In version 59, the following updates are available.

- Better OpenType features support.

- You can do this under the text>OpenType feature in the menu bar.

- Better support for variable font options such as width, weight, slant, optical size, and many more.

In version 60, one gets the following features:

- No need to visit a browser to add libraries.

- Symbols, TextStyles, and LayerStyles at a single place under the new component panel and component popover.

- Search, sort, filter become quite convenient.

- Quick search to find the exact symbol or style.

In version 61, the following features are available.

- **The component panel can see a full preview of text style:** text style name, size, and alignment.

In version 62, the following features are available.

- A better option to save on Cloud or local disk is asked when saving the Document.

- A minimum standard is considered to be set for smart layout button; it does not let the size of the control shrink. This feature is available in the Inspector section, where you can select horizontal or vertical layouts.

In version 63, the following enhancement is available.

- You can upload Sketch documents to the Cloud at a faster rate.

In version 64, the following updates took place.

- Symbols and Styles are now easier to search. A fuzzy search is available, which means you don't have to type the exact words to search. The search bar is visible on the top bar of the component panel, component menu, and layer list.

- One of the features introduced in this version is **tints;** using this one does not need to rely on complex work-around and multiple layer styles. They provide easier overriding, which makes them better at creating icons for various states. They work more efficiently with single color symbols and groups that utilize multiple opacities. The new tints option is found in the style heading in the Inspector section.

- **Redesigned component menu:** They had made it easier to search between components from the same group or every other library in the Document. In this version, they have also brought back the old menus.

In version 65, they have introduced a new feature that maintains the scroll position after click. In this version, you can also create overlay style elements and state changes.

In version 66, nothing new is introduced; only some bugs are fixed and improved.

In version 67, working around complex symbols is now more responsive. There is also improvement in background blur and saturation around shadows and layers.

In this version, also they introduced inserting the font files in the individual documents. This can be done by going to text>Document; then you have to select the font you want to embed in the Document.

In version 68, a new feature that works as a helping hand. The assistant feature is introduced in this version. They are better at spotting issues, stay consistent with the design system, and nothing much is presented in this version.

In version 69, the following features were introduced.

- **Color variable:** This feature helps us apply solid color to the fills, borders, or anywhere. On editing the color variable, you will notice changes in every part of the Document. It replaces solid color presets. There is also an option for a new color variable in the color popover.

- This version also introduced the component view for local symbols, text style, layer styles, and color variables. This way, organizing and adjusting their properties is more straightforward.

- There is also another feature called insert window, where you will be able to insert components faster separately.

In version 70, they introduced the UI redesigned for the new macOS Big Sur design language. A new toolbar is presented in this version, and one can change the toolbar item by clicking view > customize the toolbar. Nothing more has been changed to this version.

In version 71, they have introduced a bunch of features in this update.

- The user can highlight the critical update and also manage who can see the entire version history.

- One can apply JSON data sources to set information to their design.

In version 72.1, the following updates are available.

- Version 72.1 was a performance update version.

- **Data management:** Whether you want to pick data at random or not, you can use the data menu for the purpose. There is also support to nested data within linked data.

In the upcoming versions 73, 74.1, and 75, nothing much updated except the document setting window.

Sketch has improved its features over the years, and the latest version, 76, was released on August 31, 2021. It requires macOS Catalina (10.15.0) or a newer version.

In the latest version, you will get the following:

- Undo support in the new document setting window for changes made to font panels and canvas.

- While zoom in, you will get improved visibility.

- Improved error reporting while importing invalid data-linked sources.

You will get some of the issues fixed in the updated version, such as

- The layer issue not appearing on Mac OS 10.15 is resolved in this version.

- Outer borders applied to bitmaps not visible on canvas are fixed.

- The layer list not appearing correct after switching between light and dark mode on macOS 10.15 is resolved.

- Incorrect preview in insert windows is resolved.

- Document refuses to open or hang Sketch for a while is resolved.

- Copying SVG code from a selected layer could result in an error, and an incorrect ingredient is fixed.

- Toggling toolbar visibility not persistent between app launches and opened documents issue is resolved.

DOWNLOAD AND INSTALLATION

For downloading the Sketch app for macOS, you need to visit their official website sketch.com and register yourself. Once you sign in, you will get an option of a free trial version for 30 days, and you can download Sketch for macOS and use the free version. Sketch 76 is the latest version available for macOS, which was released recently on August 31, 2021. It requires macOS Catalina (10.15.0) or a newer version.

Sketch is developed for macOS, and it does not support on Windows operating system.

After the free trial is over, you can purchase the standard version for $9 per editor monthly billing or $99 per editor yearly. In the standard version, you will get unlimited documents and projects, version history, shared libraries, real-time Collaboration, components, prototyping, advanced layout, customizable, work offline, view projects and papers, inspect the design, download assets, comment, and discuss. You can also go for the business version for advanced needs.

MAJOR FEATURES OF SKETCH

1. Tools Sets.

2. Plug-ins.

3. Symbols.

4. Export Presets.

5. Vector Editing.

6. Instant Preview.

7. Libraries.

8. Grids and Guides.

9. Code Export.

WHAT'S NEW?

1. You will find Workspaces where you can edit, store, and sync data across the Sketch platform.

2. Real-time Collaboration, where everyone working on the forum can see and learn from other's work.

3. There is an option for embedding artboards, documents, and prototypes in the website.

4. My draft feature for storing the Document which is not ready for use.

5. Privacy is taken care of by the use of the document permission feature.

6. Essential highlights are placed in the starred updates.

BENEFITS OF SKETCH

1. **Nondestructive editing:** Original data is not destroyed. So one can reuse the original data example image if one does not like the edited picture or data.

2. **Exportable codes and presets:** The designer can refine or use their creativity in other applications. Codes and presets are exportable.

3. **Object alignments:** Guides and Grids let the user place and move the objects around with precision. Artists can be very particular with it.

4. **Reusable elements:** Symbols allow users to create icons and other design elements. Users can save these design elements and customize them for future uses without making them again and again.

5. **Collaborative platform:** Teammates and external colleagues can collaborate. Libraries play a vital role in facilitating designers to share symbols and use symbols shared by other designers. Everyone remains updated on this platform due to this feature.

6. **Community support:** Sketch Cloud is used to post user's queries and get them resolved quickly. It does not wait for the email method, which creates a delay in solving concerns.

DOCUMENTS AND WORKSPACES

Workspace

It provides you a place to carry out your design work, store it, and sync it across the web and Mac apps. The sync data is available everywhere after you sign in to the Sketch app.

How to Open the Workspace?

Workspace is available in the document window, and if you have created a project, that will appear in the sidebar. You can open this by clicking on File>open Workspace Document. Alternatively, you can press the Ctrl + O button to open the Document.

The Document can be visible to

1. Anyone.

2. Only certain guest.

3. Only you.

You can edit the Document by clicking on the edit button.

How to Create a New Document?

You can create a new document by clicking on File>New or pressing Ctrl + N.

How to Save the Documents?

Select File>Save button to save your Document on mac or web app. Users can also do it alternatively by pressing Ctrl + S. The user will keep his copy locally. You can also choose the Collaborate button in the toolbar, choose a project and workspace, and click on the Save button. The user will collaborate your workspace with the project.

When working with other people, you can download the workspace and edit it to make necessary changes and manually upload it to your workspace. By doing this, you will create a new version of the Document. It generally asks for confirmation as you might overwrite edits from other editors. But when you are offline and someone deletes the changes you made, changes won't apply to the Document.

Deleting Updates

Open the Document and go to the update to be deleted, then select triple dots(…) and choose delete. You cannot delete if there is only one update.

Switching between Workspaces

All the workspaces appear on the top left side of the mac and web app's document window. All you can do is to toggle between the workspaces by scrolling down the cursor. You can also do this by pressing Ctrl + 1.

View Workspace Document in Web App

It is elementary to see the workspace in the mac app just by clicking on File>Workspace.

If you want to view it in the browser, click on the three dots and select view in the browser; you will see the workspace. If the Document is shared via email, you can find it in the drop-down menu in the left sidebar.

Exploring Web App Version

There are two options to browse documents in a web app that are list view or grid view. You can use the arrow key on the left side to jump between the papers.

Artboard can be viewed in full size by zoom in to 100%. You have to press keys for the following function:

1. 0 – zoom to 100%.

2. 1 – fit Artboard on screen.

3. +/- – used for zoom in and zoom out.

Local Copy of the Document

In the mac app, you can select File > Duplicate for making a duplicate copy or local copy.

You can also do this by choosing File > Save As.

In the web app, you can do this by clicking on Download Document in the workspace.

Moving Document from My Draft to Shared Place

The web app is done by hovering over the thumbnail and clicking on three dots and then selecting move to project; you shall choose the project where you want to move the Document.

Preview Thumbnail to Document

The Artboard shall be at least 250 × 250 for the thumbnail to show.

How to Download Documents from a Web App?

One can download the Document by hovering over to the Document, clicking on three dots, and selecting the download document option.

How to Rename the Documents?

In the mac app, you can do this by selecting File > Rename.

You need to hover over the Document from the web app, click on three dots, and select Rename.

In the artboard view, click on setting, then select Rename.

How to Delete the Document?

If you are working on the Mac app, you just need to click on the thumbnail in the Document window and select delete document. But if you are using the web app, you need to hover over the thumbnail, click on the three dots and select the Delete Document option. Alternatively, dragging the Document to trash also works.

If you are using artboard view, then you need to click on setting and choose Delete Document.

How to Restore the Documents?

You need to visit the trash, hover over the Document's preview, click on the three dots, and select Restore Document. Simultaneously, you can permanently delete the Document from the trash.

CONCLUSION

In this chapter, we understood the overview of Sketch. We learned about the history of Sketch from its release in 2010 and getting better in the later version with enhanced features. We took a glimpse of version 76 and the prerequisite for its installation.

We learned the significant features of Sketch. The Sketch app has many benefits, and we got familiar with some of them. We saw the installation process of the Sketch app. It's a free trial version and then how to purchase a standard version for individuals.

CHAPTER 2

The Sketch Interface

IN THIS CHAPTER

- ➤ To acquire fundamental knowledge about the Sketch Interface

- ➤ Understanding the different functions performed on the Canvas

- ➤ Getting familiar with the fundamentals of the Toolbar

- ➤ Understanding the Layer List

- ➤ Visualizing the Component View

In this chapter, our objective is to learn the Sketch Interface. It is the place that developers use to interact with the

DOI: 10.1201/9781003261575-2

application. It has many essential components such as The Canvas, The Toolbar, The Layer List, The Component View, The Inspector, and The Insert Window. In this chapter, we will discuss various features that are relevant to the design process.

Sketch has a dark and a light mode in which you can work. You can change the mode from the setting menu. The Sketch Interface has a navigation bar on the left side which is very important for checking projects and knowing workspace details. There is a toolbar which appears at the top of the Window through which you can insert different things such as data, images, etc. It contains the zoom level where you can perform the zoom in and zoom out function. It provides you with the Group/Ungroup option to group/ungroup data as per the design requirements. That will be important from the context of Layers. In Sketch, you can customize the Interface. If you want to check the alignment, you can also create Rulers on the Interface, which helps you do so. It also provides you options to work with Grids, Layouts, and various other creations. You can customize the Toolbar. You can also add new elements in the Toolbar by the drag and drop method. You can add spacing between the new components. It is possible to customize the whole Interface according to what suits your design and make it better.

On the left side of the Interface, you can see the Layer List, which is the most used element in the Sketch Interface. It contains all the artboards, including your screens, buttons, text, images, and all other related things with which you are working. An artboard includes elements such as a smooth corner layer to make your corner smooth, groups, and backgrounds.

In the Interface at right side, you will find the Inspector. It lets us do multiple things with the layers. Suppose you select some Artboard from the layer list; you can find their details in the Inspector, such as the position of your Layer, amount of the turning degree, width, and height. You can adjust the size of the Artboard. It lets us set the opacity in percentage. It also provides you the option to set different blending modes. Along with the primary Color, you can also add a gradient color to add styles. You can also remove intensity or opacity if you wish to.

The Inspector in the Sketch Interface lets you work with borders such as inside borders or outside borders. You can set border color, width, and reset the size of the border for overall customization. It also lets you work with Shadows and inner Shadows. You can also work with a blur; typically, you have a usual blur and background blur. You can set the amount of fill color.

Once you select an Artboard, you get an option to preview it and also export it.

When you start a new document in Sketch, you will find blank spaces. You have to add an Artboard by clicking on the insert button and then selecting Artboard. The Artboard will appear in the pages section. In the pages section, you will have your page1 and symbols. We will talk about symbols later on. If you have to design a logo for a company, then you need to create the following:

1. A new page called logo or company icon.

2. Another page for the App Design.

3. Another page for the website.

4. And if you need to create a business card, then create a separate page for that.

After creating the pages, you need to develop artboards. Here, you can make an artboard of a rectangle shape and then reshape it to the phone's size. It would help if you had predetermined values such as sizes. These can vary according to the size of the phone, such as an iPhone. In-app pages, you can start designing your Artboard. You can create a new element such as a rectangle in the Artboard that will act as a button. You can adjust or customize its value to make it appear like a button. It is possible to add new layers. One can add a new layer through the Internet and drag them in. You also have an option of predetermined elements such as for iPhone x4-10. It is necessary to add a status bar to the Artboard. The different functions can be performed to the Layer like change styles, copy it, etc. It is possible to add custom colors to the button. You can add an image to the Layer and mask it in the controller itself by right-clicking on the button in the navigation bar and selecting the mask option.

THE CANVAS

The canvas is one of the essential parts of the design workflow. It is the whole area which you use to design. It is used for creating Artboards. You can enable the rulers to check how big the canvas area is. The area starts from 0,0 on the horizontal and vertical axis and goes up to infinitely large on the horizontal and vertical axis. You need to set the drag the object to select the position on the ruler. Alternatively, you can use Ctrl + R to make the ruler visible or hide them. It is challenging to find pixels while you zoom in, but only grids appear in the background. We already discussed in the previous chapter that Sketch works on the vector principle and not the pixels. So you will get a sharp image even when you zoom in to a large extent. But if you need to view pixels, then you need to click on the view pixels button. This is not recommended, although as it makes the image appear blurry.

If you need to show a grid or layout, click on the view menu and then select canvas, then you need to click on the show Grid or show layout button. The Grid or layout will appear in the Interface. The Grid has a setting to define the grid block size and define the thick lines. Showing configuration turns out to be helpful, especially when you are designing the website. You can specify settings for columns and rows. You can also define the total width of the Artboard. It is possible to offset many columns. Columns are usually used to align things. Users can also use the lines on the rulers for alignment with our content. If you want to hide some Sketch files, then drag them out of the canvas, and this way, you can delete them. If you want to create a new line, go on the ruler cursor and select the points where you want to make the lines. It is a straightforward process.

So we have seen how we can create the Grid or layout and how we can align them with our content.

Navigation in the Canvas and Zoom Feature

If you want to navigate around the canvas, you need to press the space bar and click and drag around the canvas.

You could zoom in and zoom out by holding the Ctrl + mouse scroll. User can also be done by using the pinch gesture on the trackpad, or you can also use the zoom option in the Toolbar. Users can also do it by pressing the Z in the zoom tool and pressing the zoom in or Alt keys to zoom out. You can zoom a specific area by enabling the zoom tool just by dragging a selection to zoom.

The available zoom shortcuts keys are

1. Ctrl + 0 for zooming to 100%,

2. Ctrl + 1 will zoom in to see the whole canvas,

3. Ctrl + 2 for selected layers,

4. Ctrl + 3 for center layers,

5. Ctrl+ for zoom-in feature, and

6. Ctrl- for the zoom-out feature.

Show Pixels on Canvas

The Canvas, by default, works on the vector, so zooming will not affect your work. You can zoom in to any level and still see a sharp image. Layers are measured in point when you are working on a mac app; you will have one issue equal to one pixel on the Canvas.

As we have understood earlier also that if it's necessary to show pixels, then it can be done by selecting **View > Canvas > Show Pixels on Zoom**, or you can alternatively press Ctrl + P and that will enable pixel zoom where you can see the individual pixel when you cross 100%.

Pixels Grid

The next question which appears in our mind is how we can see the pixel Grid. Users can do it by selecting **View > Canvas > Show Pixel Grid on Zoom**, or you can also press Ctrl + X to see the nonaligned edges of the layers. It is clearly visible once you pass 600%.

Rulers

The rulers are hidden by default in mac app, but you can enable them by pressing **View > Canvas > Show Rulers** or alternatively by pressing the Ctrl + R button.

You can set the zero origins anywhere on canvas where you like your Artboard to begin and define the end origin. You can also reset your ruler origin by simply clicking on **View > Canvas > Reset Ruler Origin**.

Guides Creation

By clicking anywhere on the ruler, you can create Guides. These are visible when your rulers are on. By moving layers on canvas, then it will automatically snap to the nearest Guide.

By clicking and dragging inside the ruler, you can move the Guide. To delete the Guide, you drag it to the Inspector or the Layer list until the cursor changes; it will delete the Guide.

How Can Grids Be Created?

There are two types of Grid available in the mac app: a regular grid(square Grid) and a layout grid. Users can view them at the same time.

For creating the square Grid, you need to press **View > Canvas > Show Grid**, or alternatively, you can also press the Ctrl + G button. To change the thickness of the lines, size of cells, you can open **View > Canvas > Grid Setting** and perform the required changes. The same Ctrl + G button is used in hiding the Grid.

For creating a layout Grid, you need to select **View > Canvas > Layout Setting**. From there, you can select the requisite number of rows and columns, width, gutter widths, and their colors.

The Grid is applicable only on canvas or the Artboard. You can apply the Grids on the multiple Artboards at the same time. There is also the option of edit available. You can hide or show the layout Grids by pressing the same button Ctrl + L.

How to Measure the Distance between Different Layers?

By selecting the first Layer, pressing the Alt key, and hovering over the Layer, you wish the distance between, you can measure their length. If that Layer is inside a Grid, you need to press the Ctrl button as well. Alt will also measure the distance to the text layer.

The Color of the measuring Guides is changed by selecting the Canvas tab in the preference.

THE TOOLBAR

Let us learn how to use Toolbar and customize Toolbar. Depending on the convenience, you can keep the icon, text, and icon & text in the toolbar menu. It is used to store all the different elements like vector, pencil, text, image, etc. It is straightforward to add elements in the Toolbar from the menu. It lets you drag and drop the elements to the toolbar section from the toolbar menu. It is also removed similarly. There is also an option to restore your Toolbar to the default one by simply dragging the default toolbar in the toolbar section.

For **Customizing toolbar**, you need to click on **View > Customize Toolbar**. Here are some of the functions of the default toolbar:

1. It is easy to Switch between **Component view and Canvas view**.

2. You can add different layers to Canvas by using **the Insert +** button.

3. It lets you **Create Symbols**. You can convert a group or Layer into reusable symbols. It enables you to choose a name and layout when you create a new symbol.

4. It lets you move within the layer list and organize different layers. You can do so by the Forward, Backward, Group, and Ungroup options in the Toolbar. This makes Sketch more organized.

5. Edit option lets you edit.

6. It lets you perform different Boolean operations such as Union, Subtract, Intersect, and Difference.

7. It lets you use **the View** option, which shows the design appearance on canvas.

8. The preview option is also one of the significant features. It is helpful during the prototyping.

9. You can use **Collaborate** option to add documents to the workspace.

10. If there are any Library updates, you will know this through the notification option.

11. Toggling between hide/show toolbar can be done using the Ctrl + Alt + T button and also by **View > Show/Hide Toolbar.**

THE LAYER LIST

The Layer List consists of all Artboards, Pages, and layers. You can rename or reorder the components in the Layer List.

In section, we are going to learn different operations which you can perform on the Layer List.

Hide and Lock Layers

For hiding a layer in the Layer List, you need to hover over to the layer name and click on the eye icon. Your name will conceal. But if the eye icon already appears when you hover over the word, it means the Layer is already hidden. You can use the shortcut keys to toggle between the show/hide layer by pressing the ⌘ + ⇧ + H key. This will perform that function.

Now come Locking the Layer; for that, you need to hold ⌥ and hover over to the item you want to lock, then click on the padlock icon. Your Layer will be closed. For unlocking, you need to click again on the padlock icon. Alternatively, you can press ⌘ + ⇧ + L for the lock/unlock feature. You have to remember that you cannot edit or move a layer when you lock a layer.

Using Pages

Pages let you organize your work and improve efficiency with complex documents. You can use any number of Pages you would like to.

It is straightforward to create a new page; you just need to click on the + icon, which appears on top of Layer List. You shall give an appropriate name to your page. You can navigate between the pages in the Layer list itself, or alternatively, you can press Fn + ↑ or Fn + ↓ to move up and down between the pages. You can also use this(>) to collapse the pages. Users could use the Dropdown menu for navigation.

You can also change the order of pages by just dragging them. Alternatively, you can use Ctrl-click on the pages to make a duplicate copy or delete them.

It is also possible to drag Artboards or Layers within the Layer List across various pages.

Using Artboards

Artboards are used to create a fixed frame on the Canvas. They have significant use in designing the screen size or any specific device. They are optional features. It is elementary to create Artboard, you need to click on **Insert > Artboard** on the Toolbar, or alternatively, you can also do this by pressing the Ctrl + A. A custom-size Artboard can also be created by clicking and dragging on the Canvas or by choosing a preset from the Inspector. For saving the Artboard as preset, click on the + button in the Inspector and provide it a proper name.

Once you created an Artboard, you can duplicate it by pressing the Ctrl + D button.

How to Move Artboard?

You can move an Artboard by selecting it. If it has no layers inside it, you are free to click anywhere on it. But if it has a layer, you need to click on the title on Canvas or select the title from the Layer List. Users can change the value of X and Y in the Inspector by dragging around Canvas and using arrow keys to move it.

Resize Artboards

You need to click, select, and drag on the selection handle to resize an Artboard. It is also convenient to edit its dimensions in the Inspector. At the same time, you can also resize content on Artboard by selecting **Adjust content on resize** in the Inspector. It is also necessary to resize constraints within layers.

You can also select a fit option in the Inspector to automatically resize the content. In the next section, we will look at how to delete an Artboard.

Delete the Artboard

You need to select the Artboard which you wish to delete, then press the backspace key. This will delete the layers within an Artboard. It is also possible to keep the Artboard content and delete the Artboard; you need to select the Artboard and click on ungroup. Alternatively, you can do this via pressing ⌘ + ⇧ + G.

Searching in the Layer List

If your document consists of lots of layers and you want to search a particular layer, you can do so by using the search bar at the top of the Layer List. You need to enter the specific layer name to search it.

Note that Layers with long names are truncated in the Layer List. You can see the full View of the trimmed Layer by hovering over its truncated part.

THE COMPONENTS VIEW

The component View lets you create, manage, search, and find local elements, Layer styles, Text Styles, and color variables.

How to Access It?

You can access the component view by clicking on the components tab, which appears on the left side of the Toolbar. Alternatively, you can also press Ctrl + 1 and Ctrl + 2 to switch between the Components View and the Canvas View.

There are four Components View types that Users can view by pressing the center button in the Toolbar. These views are Symbols, Text Styles, Layer Styles, and Color Variables.

How to Work in Component View?

1. **Switch views:** It lets you toggle between the Component View and the Canvas. We had seen earlier in this chapter how Users can do it.

2. **Filter components:** By default, you can use the Symbols, but you can use the Toolbar to switch between other components such as Symbols, Text Styles, Layer Styles, and Color Variables.

3. **Edit in the Inspector:** It lets you delete, edit, or rename any Symbol, Layer Styles, Text Styles, etc. Users can do this by selecting the Component and making the requisite changes.

4. **Search:** Select the component types and then search for the component name.

5. **Create a new layer or duplicate:** you can create a new layer, Text Style, or Color Variable. For this, you need to press on + button on the toolbar menu. It is also possible to duplicate symbols with the help of a toolbar where a duplicate icon is present. You need to click on that.

6. **Contextual menu:** you need to press Ctrl and click on the component thumbnail to rename, create, copy, or delete their CSS attribute. All of the operations are performed using a contextual menu.

7. **Insert+:** You can use Insert to add some part or Component to the Canvas. For this, you need to click on the Component and then select the + button; it lets you drop the Component into the Canvas.

The component view is essential for organizing. It shows only the local components of the document. It does not even show components that are inserted from the libraries. For managing that library component, you need to open the original library Sketch file.

Create a New Component using Component View

It is elementary to create Components such as new Text Style, Layer Styles, and color variables using the component view.

The process to develop the different Component looks very similar; still, you shall look at individual instruction for each Component.

Create Text Styles

Text Styles lets you create a different set of Styles and enables you to use them in different text layers within the designs. You can apply changes to the Text Layer in particular or apply changes to all Text Layers simultaneously.

You need to select that Text Layer on which you applied Styles, then select **Layer > Create new Text Style** from the menu. Alternatively, you can also go to the Inspector section, and then you will find the No Text Style Section and a + button below it. You need to click on the + button, type a new name to your Text Style and save it. This will also create a unique Text Style.

If you want to do this from the Component view, you need to click on the + or Create Text Style Aa in the Toolbar, and after that, you can edit the properties in the Inspector.

Apply a Text Style

For applying a Text Styles, you need to follow the following steps:

1. Select a layer.

2. Under the Appearance section in the Inspector, you will find No Text Style as the pop-up menu; you need to click on that. You need to select the Text Style from the components to popover and apply it. The search bar helps you find the Styles.

Alternatively, Users can also do this by using Insert Window. It would help if you chose Window > Insert or press C to open the window menu. You have to select the Text Styles tab Aa and choose the Styles you want to use in your document. Alternatively, you can do the drag and drop in the empty space on the canvas to create that Style.

You can use **Insert Text with Style** from the component view panel.

Edit a Text Style

Once you have applied the Text Style and made the necessary changes, you will find that an asterisk(*) appears beside Style's name. There you can perform various operations such as:

1. **Update:** It will make changes to The Layers.

2. **Create+:** It will create a new Text Style, and you can also apply changes to it.

3. **Detach:** It basically removes the Text Style but keeps the changes that you made to the Layers.

4. **More(…):** It lets you with the option to reset the Styles or rename them.

Text Styles is edited using the Component View. For that, you first need to switch to the Components View and then select the Text Styles tab in the Toolbar. You can change/ edit the Style in the Inspector section on the right side. It will automatically apply to all of the Layers using that Text Style in the document.

Text Styles can also be included as part of the Library and can be shared with others.

Layer Style

It works similarly to the Text Style. The only difference is that in Text Style, you need to work with text layers, while in Layer Styles, you need to work with Shape Layers.

For creating a Layer Style, you need to select the Shape Layer on which Styles are applied. You need to click on **Layer > Create new Layer Style.** Alternatively, you can do this using Component View, you need to open Component View, and then select +/Create Layer Style from the toolbar menu. It follows a similar process as what we did in the Text Style.

It can also be included as part of the Library and can be shared with others.

There are two ways to insert a Text or Layer Style as a new layer:

1. Users can do it via **Insert Window.** It is done by pressing the C button or selecting the **Window > Insert** in the insert menu +. You need to select the Layer Style, then search for the Style you want to insert Window and drag and drop onto Canvas to create a new layer.

2. The other method through which we can insert a Text or Layer Style is the **Component View.** If you want to do it from here, then you select the Component which you want to insert as a New Layer and then click on **insert Shape with Style.** For text, you need to click on **Text with Style** in the Inspector.

. Alternatively, Users can also insert it from the Toolbar menu. It is a similar process, and you need to select Layer Style or Text Style, which you want to apply. Click anywhere on Canvas to insert that Style.

Create Color Variable

It lets you set Color and use it across your documents by sync feature. The changes made to the Color Variable will appear across all of the Layers that use it. You can create a color variation that is local to specific documents or share them in Library.

Here are some of the features of the Color Variables:

1. It lets you keep the designs in an organized manner and also speeds the workflow.

2. The sync feature is a unique property, and when you apply changes to a Color Variable, then it will apply to other Layers that use it.

3. Existing global Color presets are part of Color Variables that is in its Library.

There is also support to Color Variables in the Inspector.

I will show you the following two methods using; you can create a Color Variable:

1. Creating it **from the Inspector section:** Select the Layer, then click on the Inspector section's Color well. Please select the Color you want to use, click on the Create Color Variable button, and don't forget to give it a name.

2. Creating it **from the Components View:** You need to switch to Component mode, then select the Color tab from the Toolbar. Then click on Create Color Variable or + button. Please select the color and give it a name and then save it.

Organize Color Variables

You need to switch to Component View and then go to the Colors tab. You need to hold ⇧ and select all the Variables which you want to group. You can also rename the group from the left sidebar. You can also bring Color Variables in the existing groups which appear on the left side. You can simply do drag and drop.

You can group Color Variables by adding a/in their names. It is similar to Symbols or Text Styles. Before/things will be the group names, and after the slash/these is part of the Component name within that group.

For example, Primary/dark and Primary/light belong to the same group Primary within Components dark and light.

You can group Color Variables **using Component View.** Color variables and the group will arrange themselves automatically in alphabetical order.

To apply Color variables to a Layer.

Three different methods can do this. I will list down all three essential strategies:

1. Apply it **from the Inspector section:** It lets you apply from Inspector by two methods. The first is to select that Layer on which Color Variable has to be used, and then you can choose any color variable from the Grid in the Color well. The second method to apply

it is by clicking on the color swatch icon next to the color well icon. These will let you use Color Variable successfully.

2. Apply it **from the Insert Window:** for doing this, you need to click on **Windows > Components.** Alternatively, you can use the C on the keyboard. There is a Color tab that appears in the left sidebar. You can use a simple drag and drop feature to apply a color swatch to any Layer. Users can also drop color Variables in the color wells in the fills in the Inspector Section.

3. Apply it **from the Find and Replace menu:** You can use the find and replace menu, click on the Color well next to "replace with" and choose the color variable you want to apply.

Edit Color Variable

It can again be done by the Inspector section, Component View, and Find and Replace method. It is easy to copy HEX, RGB, HSL, Objective-C simply by clicking the Color Variable.

I will show you two ways how you can edit a Color Variable. These are

1. Edit it **from the Inspector:** Select the Layer and click on the Color well in the Inspector sidebar. Click on the edit Variable and choose a new Color. Then press the Update button to save the changes. Only those Color variables which are local to the document can be edited. For editing the library Color Variable, you need to edit this from the Library document.

2. Do it using **The Component View:** You need to change to Component View, then click on the Colors tab. Click on the Color which you want to edit and select a new Color from the Inspector. It will automatically save the changes.

Rename a Color Variable

User can do this by switching to the Component View and then selecting the Colors tab. Select the swatch you want to rename. Assign a new name under the Inspector section. Changes will be saved automatically.

Delete a Color Variable

Again you need to switch to Component View and select the Colors tab. Select the color swatch and hit the backspace button to delete the Color Variable.

Detach Color Variable

If you want to make changes to a single Layer without updating the Color Variable itself, you need to detach Color variables first. You can do this using the Inspector sidebar. You need to select the Layer you want to separate, go to Color well in the Style menu in the Inspector, and click on Detach Variables.

Find or Replace Color Variable

You can do this using the **Edit menu > Find and Replace Color** or press this ⌘ + ⌥ + F to open the Find and Replace dialogue box.

Now we have seen how to create a Text Style, Layer Style, and Color Variable. Users cannot make symbols in the Component View, but Users can duplicate them. You can also edit the symbol source in the Inspector bar.

How to Organize Components?

We have seen how component view makes it easier to organize and manage your Components.

We have also seen how we select the multiple Components and group them using Ctrl + G or choosing the group option after selecting them. You can also rename the existing group. If you want to rename a single Component, you can do this by using the name field in the Inspector.

Expand and Collapse Group

Users can collapse all of the groups by choosing **View > Sidebar > Collapse All Groups**.

THE INSPECTOR

The Inspector is one of the essential parts of the Sketch Interface. It consists of the setting of any layers selected or control for the tool you want to use. It can hide and show the control depending on your requirement.

The Inspector consists of the following:

1. **Alignment option:** It becomes active when we select two or more layers. We will learn about aligning techniques in the upcoming chapter.

2. **Layer properties:** They let you change the size, position, and rotation of the Layer and provide the option to flip the Layer.

3. **Radius:** It lets you smooth or round the corner in the rectangle or square. We will see in detail about the editing radius.

4. **Resizing Constraints:** All the control which you have selected within Artboard or Layer is visible. We will learn about resizing Constraints in the next chapter.

5. Prototyping allows you to add a target Artboard in the prototypes and fix the Layer while scrolling and animate the Layer.

6. **Appearance:** It lets you create, update, or detach your layer styles.

7. **Style:** It lets you control how your Layer looks. You can add a new style by clicking on adding a unique style. You can hide the Style which is added by deselecting the checkbox next to them. To remove any styles altogether, you need to deselect its checkbox, and you need to click on the trash which appears. We will see the styling later on.

8. We will learn about exporting in detail later on in the upcoming topic.

THE INSERT WINDOW

It is different from the main Window. It lets you find and insert symbols, Layer Styles, Text Styles, and Color variables. It shows you a preview, which Users can use to drag and drop in the Canvas.

The User can open the Window using the shortcut key C, or alternatively, you can choose **Window > Insert**. Toggling between the Components is possible in the sidebar of the Window. You can filter between the libraries and local components.

For navigating the Insert Window, you can do this by following:

1. **Components tab:** It let you filter between Text Styles, Layer Style, Symbols, and Color Variables.

2. **Search bar:** It will show you the result for the Component type you have selected in the sidebar. It would help if you were sure to select the relevant component type. Else it won't work.

3. **Sidebar:** It lets you navigate between different libraries and groups and filter previews on the right side.

4. **Previews:** You get better previews for each Component. You can also drag and drop the previews in the Canvas.

5. **Window pinning:** By default, the Insert Window hides behind the document window. To make the Insert Window reappear, you need to click on the icon simply.

Inserting Components from Insert Window

To insert a Component, you need to first search for the components such as Symbols, Text Styles, Layer Styles, or Color Variable. The components will appear in the sidebar, and you need to select the type of the relevant Component.

Select the Symbol, Text Styles, or anything else, and you need to drag and drop in the Canvas simply. To apply, you need to drag and drop the Symbols. Similarly, for Color Variable, you need to select the fill from the Inspector section.

It is easy to switch between the Components types by pressing the ⌘ + 1, ⌘ + 2, ⌘ + 3, ⌘ + 4 keys.

EDITING SHAPES

In the Inspector section, we were discussing editing the radius. We will learn how we can edit the Shapes in the Inspector. You will find the option to edit the Shape in the Inspector once you select the Shape. The star button lets you choose the radius and number of points.

For rounding the corner of the rectangle, you need to select the rounded rectangle to adjust its corner radius, and Users can do this from the Inspector.

In Vector Editing mode, you can adjust a single corner's radius.

Flip Shapes

Users can flip the Shapes both horizontally or vertically in the Inspector. They stay selected unless you flatten the Shape, and Users can do this by choosing **Layer > Combine > Flatten**.

Now the next thing we are going to learn is how to rotate shapes. For this, you need to enter the value in degree in the Inspector. Its value can be positive or negative, and accordingly, the shapes rotate in the clockwise or anti-clockwise direction.

Alternatively, you can select the Shape and rotate using the rotate symbol in the Toolbar.

You can also change the axis on which the shapes rotates. For this, you need to click and drag the crosshair at the center.

Lastly, you can rotate the Shape by first selecting the Shape and holding ⌘ and dragging the handles.

It is also possible to rotate the Shape to a 0-degree value by choosing the **Layer > Combine > Flatten.**

Editing Shapes in Vector Editing Mode

For this, you need to double click on the shapes or select the Shape and press the enter key.

In vector editing mode, you will find circular points and paths connecting them. You can change the Shape by just clicking on the circular points and dragging them.

You can add a new point by hovering over the two points and clicking on Insert to insert a unique point.

The path is generally a straight line or curve. To change it from one form to another, you need to click on the path and change it.

We have already seen how to make Shape flatten.

Transform Tool

If you want to use the transform tool, then you need to choose **Layer > Transform**. You can also add transform tool via toolbar customization.

Scissor Tool

They are used to cut the path from the shapes. You need to choose the Shape and then select **Layer > Path > Scissor** to operate. Users can also do it by customizing the Toolbar. Click on the path which you want to remove. After doing all these steps, click outside the Shape.

CONCLUSION

In this chapter, we have learned the Sketch Interface and the critical role of The Canvas, The Layer List, The Component, The Color Variable, The Insert Window, and The Inspector. At last, we learned about editing Shapes.

CHAPTER 3

Layers Basics and How to Work with Them

IN THIS CHAPTER

➢ Getting familiar with the layers basics and how to work with them.

➢ We will see how to select the Layer.

➢ We will learn how to group Layer.

➢ To make the Grid.

➢ Learn aligning and resizing Layer.

➢ We will also learn smart distribution, resizing, moving, and rotating layers.

DOI: 10.1201/9781003261575-3

In the previous chapter, we learned about the Sketch Interface. We have understood important components such as the Canvas, the Toolbar, the Layer List, the Component View, etc. We have dealt with various features in the Canvas such as Navigation, show pixel grid, rulers, guides, etc. We have learned the Customization of The Toolbar. We explored various features of the Layer List. We have also seen the function of the Component View. We have understood Text Style, Layer Style, and Color variables in detail.

In this chapter, we are going to learn the basics of Layers and their working procedure. We will see how to select and group Layers. We will learn to make Grids. We will also explore aligning Layers and resizing Layers.

LAYERS BASICS AND HOW TO WORK WITH THEM

Layers act as the building block of creating Designs. There are different types of Layers such as Shapes, Groups, and Artboards.

Adding Layers

For adding Layer, click on the Insert + button in the Toolbar menu. Alternatively, Users can also do it by clicking on the insert menu in the menu bar. There are a variety of Layers available such as Shapes, vectors, pencil, text, images, Artboards, etc.

HOW TO SELECT AND GROUP LAYERS?

Click on the Layer you want to select, and you will find a selection handle around that Layer.

By clicking on its name in the Layer, the list lets you select the Layer. Users can also do it by choosing **View > Canvas > Show > Layer Selection**.

How to Select Multiple Layers?

First select the first Layer and then hold up the arrow ⇧ and select another Layer. This way, you can choose multiple Layers.

To select any Layer within the selection area, you need to click and drag on the empty space on Canvas. You can also do this by holding ⌥ and click and drag option. You need to hold, connect, and drag to add layers to the selection or remove currently selected layers.

To remove currently selected Layers, hold ⌘ while you click and drag. Within a specific Artboard, you can choose the Layer. You need to select the Artboard itself, then choose **Edit > Select > Select All in Artboard**.

How to Select Overlapping Layers?

To select the second Layer, you need to hold ⌥ this while you click and drag.

How to Create a Group of Layers?

The benefit of grouping the Layers is you can do move and resize all of them together. You can also toggle their activities and change the properties such as opacity and blend mode.

Create Group of Layers

It is done by pressing the ⌘ + G, alternatively, and you can also do this by choosing **Arrange > Group**.

Ungroup Layers

To do this, you need to press ⌘ + ⇧ + G, alternatively, and you can also choose **Arrange > Ungroup**.

How to Select a Layer in a Group?

You need to double-click on the group and then select the Layer which you want to select. Alternatively, you can also do this by pressing the Ctrl and click on the Layer within the group to choose. You need to check to enable through for new groups under the checkbox. It lets you disable across the whole document and automatically select a layer within the group. You can also do this for the individual group by choosing a group and checking select group content.

MAKING GRID

Select a layer and then choose **Arrange > Make Grid**. You can provide the number of rows and columns in the button right corner. You can also edit the spacing between the Layers. The number of cells and spacing in the Grid is also editable. It is also possible to make grids of several layers. You shall make the layers evenly aligned. You can select and drag them in the bottom corner to make the Grid.

ALIGNING AND RESIZING LAYERS

There is six alignment button in the top row of the Inspector. They are horizontal distribution, vertical distribution, align left, align horizontal, align right, align top, align vertically, and align bottom.

If two or more layers are selected, then alignment is done toward the most extensive Layer. To align Layer to a specific Layer, you need to choose that Layer and lock it using ⌘ + ⇧ + L; you need to hold up the button to keep Layer selected, then select the object you want to align.

If you need to align two or more layers on the Artboard, select your Layer, hold the Alt key, and then click on the alignment you want to use.

How to Align Multiple Layers?

The tidy button lets you align the multiple layers. The tidy button appears on the top of the Inspector. It will arrange layers evenly in rows and columns.

Smart Distribution

You can move multiple layers using the smart distribution feature. You can also make the spacing between the multiple layers, horizontal or vertical. You need to choose two or more layers and then click and drag the handle. If layers are arranged in a grid, the spacing between them can be made in a horizontal row and vertical spacing between the rows. Smart distribute features appear when the layers are evenly distributed. For fixing this issue, you can use the Tiny button or do it manually.

It is possible to swap layers. When you select layers with even spacing between them, you need to click and drag the circular handle to move within the layers. It works on whole Artboards, so rearranging is relatively easy on the Canvas.

Swapping is also possible in the grid layout, and for that, you don't need to change the number of columns and rows.

Resizing Layers

For resizing layers, you need to select the Layer and then click and drag from any point or according to the need of changing width and height. If you hold the up arrow key, then the Layer will be resized proportionately by keeping the height and width ratio unchanged. If you press the Alt key then, it will resize from the center.

How to Resize Layers in the Inspector?

It is effortless in the Inspector, and you just need to select the Layer and mention the dimension. By default, the Layer is changed from the top left corner, but it can also be changed using the following shortcuts:

1. **press l:** scale from the left.

2. **press r:** scale from the right.

3. **press t:** scale from the top.

4. **press b:** scale from the bottom.

5. **press c/m:** scale from the center or bottom.

It is also possible to use mathematical operators in the Inspector with the following:

1. **+:** Add.

2. **- :** Subtract.

3. *** :** Multiply.

4. **/ :** divide.

The percentage is used to change the dimension. For example, if there is an 860-pixel height Artboard and you set layers height to 10%, then it will become 86-pixel height.

The corner radius values are separated using the; (semi-colon) character, for example, (30;40;10;40).

Using keyboard shortcuts, one can resize layers.

1. ⌘ + →: increases width by 1px.

2. ⌘ + ←: decrease the width by 1px.

3. ⌘ + ⇧ + →: increase the width by 10px.

4. ⌘ + ⇧ + ←: decrease the width by 10px.

Moving Layers

To move a layer, you simply need to click and drag it and, for restricting it to a particular axis, hold the up arrows ⇧ while you drag.

If the Layer is underneath another layer, in that case, if you want to move it, then select that Layer and press ⌘ + ⌥ and click and drag on Canvas.

The Sketch app aligns the Layer to the adjacent one automatically. If it does not work, then you can choose **View > Canvas > Show All Guides**.

Rotating Layers

For doing this, you need to hold ⌘ and select on any handle to rotate in that direction.

Duplicate the Layer

In order to duplicate the Layer, you need to select a layer and press ⌘ + D. It will create a duplicate layer on the top of the original in the same position. Alternatively, you can hold ⌥ and drag a layer, and this will create a duplicate. By doing this, your original Layer remains in the same place.

To create a third layer while you hold ⌥ and drag a layer, then immediately press the ⌘ + D, it will create a third layer with the same offset as the duplicate one.

How to Scale a Layer?

The styles applied to remain the same while resizing the Layer. But for scaling them proportionately with the layer size, you need to choose **Layer > Transform > Scale** or press ⌘ + K.

In the Inspector, you can choose whether the Layer will resize from the center, corner, or sides. The preview is also available.

Resize Constraints

It lets you choose in the Inspector how layers behave when you resize the Group, Artboard, or Symbol of which they are part. Resizing constraint on Group, Artboard, and Symbol is shown in the Inspector by selecting that Layer.

The right side control set the edge of the parent of layer pinning to. The middle control sets stretch in Layer's height and width or stay fixed. The preview on the right side shows the behavior of the Layer accordingly.

By default, resizing of Layer is done according to their parent, including any padding.

For resizing the layer constraint on the Artboard, you need to select the Artboard and then check to adjust content on resize in the Inspector.

Fix size will keep the dimension the same regardless of resizing of the parent layers is done.

Pin to Edge

It fixes the distance between the Layer and the distinct edge regardless of how the parent layer is resized.

This is helpful, especially while you float the action button in the interface. You can pin them to the top or left, which will ensure it stays at the same distance.

STYLING

You can create or select the Style of a layer in the Inspector. There are many things in styling a layer that you can do.

You can do a set of things in styling. These are the following:

1. Fills.

2. The Color Popover.

3. Color Variables.

4. Presets.

5. Gradients.

6. Tints.

7. Border.

8. Shadows.

9. Blurs.

10. Text Styles.

11. Layer Styles.

12. Organizing Styles.

13. Tips and Tricks.

The Sketch app provides five different types of fills:

1. Solid fill.

2. Linear gradient.

3. Radial gradient.

4. Angular gradient.

5. Image fill.

Solid color fill is the default color.

You can add a new fill by click on the + fill panel. There is no limit to add fill to a layer. They all will attach one over the other. You will have the following option for each fill:

1. Enable/disable checkbox.

2. There is also a color preview cell. From here, you can change the file types or select a different color.

3. You can use Color Swatch. Using this, you can navigate through all the Color Variables in the documents.

4. There is a blending mode in which if you select anything other than usual, then the icon will change to blue.

5. You can use the solid color fill option. There is an option to copy/paste the Color's HEX value.

6. You can combine two or more fill types by changing the fill's opacity.

You can see all the fill for any selected layer by pressing the F button. You can add an image fill as well. For adding an image file, you need to click on the Color well on a fill's option and then click on the image fill button which appears on the right side of the popover.

You can choose your image from the preset at the bottom or select data from the data source. There are four different types of fills available:

1. There is fill, which helps in adjusting the Layer's width.

2. There is a fit that lets us change the image to fit the height.

3. There is a stretch that allows us stretch the width and height to fit.

4. There is Tiles option to keep the original size.

You can see the frequently viewed images by clicking on the clock icon above the image preview. You can also choose a basic pattern or noise fill from the global presets at the bottom.

You can change the fill setting for the overlapping paths. After applying fill to the shapes, you must click on the setting near the fill icon section title. You can use the odd-even rule or non-zero to fill the shapes according to the winding rule.

You can reveal the color popover by clicking on the Color well for any fill, border, and shadow. You can work with the slider to control the Color's hue and alpha. The preview options let you show the color set. You can pick any color using the eyedropper from the display, inside or outside the Sketch app. You can also access it by pressing the Ctrl + C key. The same control key lets you bring up the eyedropper tool to set the Layer's fill color. You can use the text fields to access your Color's HEX value for copy and paste work. It is also used to manually set the specific Color using the RGB and the alpha values. You can also switch from RGB to HSB, i.e., Hue, Saturation, and Brightness, or can also switch to HSL, i.e., Hue, Saturation, Lightness. You can also create a new color variable.

The alpha value returns to 100% when changed. The HEX value is in the color popover.

The next thing to discuss is the **Color Variable**. It lets you synchronize Colors throughout the documents. The changes made to Color Variable appear across all the layers that use it. You can also create a color variation that is local to your document or also share that in the library. From the library, you can use that across other designs. It also helps maintain the speed workflow and keep the documents organized. They have the properties to synchronize across the documents, and they will update any layer when you change the color Variable. There are many global Color presets which are now Color Variables, and they live in their own local library. The Color Variable is also supported in the web app Inspector. You need to hover over the Color label and click in order to copy the color value to the clipboard. You can also change the format by clicking on the arrow next to the current value and pick the format you need. For example, Obj-C or Swift.

You can see the whole path by clicking on the Color Variable in the Inspector. You can also see its name and Color value from here. You can hover over to the color label and click on it to copy all of Color's Variable values. You can also view and copy the individual values. You just have to hover over them and then click on them.

You can use the following format:

1. HEX.

2. RGB.

3. HSL.

4. NSColor(Objective-C and Swift).

5. UIColor(Objective-C and Swift).

There are three ways to create a Color Variable:

1. From the Inspector.

2. From Components View.

3. Using Find and Replace menu.

If you want to create a Color Variable from the Inspector, then you need to select a layer and click on the Color well in the Inspector menu. You can create the Color variable by specifying the Solid Color which you wish to apply. You need to name it and then save it. You can also generate Color variables by using the eyedropper tool. It can be from inside or outside of the mac app.

For creating a Color Variable from the Components view, you can do this from the color tab and click on the + icon or the color variable button. You can pick one from the Inspector and also give it a name and save that. You can save by clicking anywhere on the previews Grid.

You can organize the color Variable or group it. To do so, you need to switch to Component view and then click on the Colors tab, hold ⇧ and select all the Color Variable to be grouped. You have to do control-click on the selection and then choose the group. You can rename the group by double-clicking on the left sidebar, and then you can rename that group. The color variations can be added in a group by just drag and drop. You can use a/in names to group a Color variable in a similar manner as the Symbols or the Text. The things coming before/will be the group's names, and all the things that appear after the/will be the Component's name.

The last part to discuss is organizing Color Variable in the Components View. The organization of groups and Color Variables is usually in an alphabetical manner. If you want to use numbers in front of the Color Variables names to categorize them in number sequence, you can do this. Do whatever suits you or makes you organize better.

The next thing to discuss is how to apply a Color Variable from the Inspector. First of all, select that Layer on which you want to use a Color Variable. From the Grid in the Color well, select the Style which you wish to apply. For any documents or library in which you created Color Variables, you can switch between the Color Variables. You can use the Color Swatch option which appears next to the Color well, for applying a Color Variable.

If you create a new text layer and apply a color to a text layer, this newly created text layer will also use that Color Variable.

The next thing to learn is to apply Color Variable from the Insert Window. To open the Component Window, you need to click on the **Window > Components**. Alternatively, you can also use shortcut key C. You can use the drag and drop method to apply the Color on the Layer and you can select this from the **Colors** tab. The Colors tab appears on the left sidebar. Any Color Variable can be dropped into the Color well in the fills in the Inspector.

You can also work with the Find and Replace menu to apply a Color Variable. Go to the Find and Replace menu, choose the color well that appears next to Replace with, and select the Color Variable you want to apply. You can close the Color picker by clicking anywhere and then press the Replace button.

Similarly, you can edit the Color Variable from the three different methods that are from the following:

1. The Inspector.

2. The Component View.

3. Find and Replace menu.

You can copy the HEX, RGB, HSL, Objective-C, and Swift, by control-clicking on any Color Variable.

First of all, we will see how to edit the Color Variables from the Inspector. For doing so, you need to follow these steps:

1. Select any of the layers.

2. Go to color well in the Inspector.

3. Press on the edit Variable and choose a new Color.

4. Select Update to save.

You should keep in mind that the document for which you are applying the Color Variable should be **local**. You can edit Color Variables from a library in their library itself.

The next thing is how to edit Color Variable from the Components View. As always, here also need to switch to the Component View first, then choose the **Colors tab**. It would be best if you choose the Color Swatch which needs to be edited, then go for the new Color from the Inspector. You will see the preview of the changes made, and then it saves them automatically.

You can **rename** a color Variable. For that, you need to switch to the Component View first and then choose the **Colors** tab. You have to select the Color Swatch which you need to rename. You can type the name in the Inspector. Here also, changes made are saved automatically. You can also rename from the control-click on the Color Swatch.

The next thing to know is that you can delete a Color Variable. Here also, you need to switch to the Components View and then choose the **Colors** tab. You can delete the Swatch of the Color Variable by selecting it and pressing the backspace. Users often use a control click to delete a Color Variable.

You can also detach a Color Variable. Suppose you want to make changes to a Color of a single layer and not the complete Color Variable then, in such a scenario, you need to detach that color variable first. You can detach a Color Variable from the Inspector. You need to select that Layer you want to detach, then go to the Color well in the Inspector and hit the detach variable option. Your color variable will be separated.

You can also find and replace a specific Color Variable or Color by choosing the **Edit > Find and Replace Color**. Alternatively, you can press ⌘ + ⌥ + F. Once the Find and Replace menu opens, you can select the Color Variable which you want within the design. You can find colors with different alphas but the same RGB or HEX value by enabling all opacities of the Color.

If you want those different alphas intact when you replace the Color, then you need to enable the original preserve opacity. The new feature introduced is the Color Variable Migrator plugin that makes it easy to apply Color Variable to layers and Styles.

I would like to tell you in brief about the Color migrator plugin. These features to migrate your Style and layers to use new Color variables were introduced in Sketch 69. You can apply this to the whole document and with maintaining consistency and update easily. The pre-69 Color Swatches were used to convert the document to the Color Variable. You have to decide whether you want to use the Color Variable and wish to migrate the layers or styles. But this problem is solved in the new version as it does help to do two things:

1. The existing Color Variable is used in all the layers.

2. It also updates all the Layers and Text Styles to use existing Color variables.

It should be noted that the current features work in the documents opened currently. You can also use them in the shared libraries, but you need to open them first.

PRESETS

You can create quick access for image fill and store gradient. It can be reused in the documents as part of the library. Solid Color presets which used to appear here have now become the Color Variable. I will let you understand how we can add the preset. For that, you need to select the image fill or gradient. You can add it to your local document as well as the global presets; click on the + icon. You should view your presets in the list view if you want to rename them. You can rename it by control-clicking on it. You can move or copy presets between the local and global documents using the same control-click method.

You can reorder them by dragging the presets, and if you want to delete them, then you need to drag them entirely out of the color popover. Alternatively, you can control-click on them and choose to delete them.

It is straightforward to create library presets. If you make a document library after saving them, it will appear in the presets menu below global and documents items. When there is any update in the presets, then a small dot appears, which tells us that they have been updated.

GRADIENT

Now in this section, I will talk about gradient fill which you can apply to a layer. You need to go to the Inspector section and then choose the color button in the fills section. You will have three options to select, i.e., linear or angular, or angular button gradients that appear at the top of the popover.

We will now learn how to create linear gradients. Using this, we can add a line to two points in a layer. You can choose a color popover in the Inspector menu to change the color on the gradient. You need to select any of the two points and then select any color. You can add a new point by clicking anywhere in the gradient, and this will add another color to the gradient. You can change the look of the gradient by dragging the color points. You can choose to delete a point by selecting it and pressing the backspace button.

We have seen the linear gradient and now moving to a radial gradient. It is very similar to the linear gradient. The only difference is one of the points now sets the middle of the effect, and at the end, its opposite points sets. You can control the size of the effect by dragging the noncolor point.

We will now learn how to create an angular gradient. It helps you place color points you make on the circle. It takes maximum height and maximum width into consideration. You can adjust their position by dragging the points. You can choose to add new points by clicking on the circle. Besides using the gradient point on the Layer, you can also use the gradient bar in the color popover. It lets you adjust and control the gradient. It has a no different approach to work, but instead, it works in a similar way. You can click anywhere on the bar to add a new color, drag to move it, and click on any point to change its Color. You can remove a point by selecting it and pressing the backspace button. Now we will learn how to adjust the gradient points with shortcuts. I will list down the following shortcuts to adjust the gradients:

1. **1 – 9:** It lets you set a new point along the gradient bar. E.g., Three sets it to 30%.

2. **=:** It enables you to position the gradient point equally between the two points.

3. **Tab:** It lets you switch between the two color points.

4. → or ←: It enables you to adjust the point position incrementally.

5. ⇧ + → or ←: It enables you to adjust the color point position in larger increments.

TINTS

It has its specific function, such as lets you apply a single color to an entire group or Symbol. It's not like the fill, and it also respects the semi-filled elements with different opacities and borders. If you want to show different states through a change in Color, then tints are an excellent option for things like complex icons or tabs in the navigation bar. Only when you select a group of Layers or a Symbol instance, you get the opportunity to use the tints. You need to click on the + icon in the Inspector if you want to add a tint to any group or any instances. It is almost similar to fills. You can change the overall color opacity or change the hex code according to your requirements. In tints, you can only use any solid color. One of another best features is to use Tints as overrides. You need to use default tints to any Symbols or instances if you wish to apply tints as overrides with nested Symbols. You have to do this on the Symbols sources you are working with. Let's say you want to use a tab bar where each tab is its own nested Symbol. You have to go to its source, more precisely the tab bar source and then apply tints to each tab Symbol instance. You will find a color item that will appear right to each Symbol's name in the Inspector when you will view the tab bar Symbol instance. You can override the default tints for each Symbol by clicking on the Symbol instance. It will bring up the color picker.

BORDERS

There is no limit to adding borders to the layers. You can add a border with the different adjustments, such as different colors, thickness, and blend modes. The most interesting thing about the borders is that they can be linear, radial, angular gradient fill, and solid Color. You can press B to show/hide the border on any layer.

You can also set the position of the border. In the case of closed shapes, you can keep the border at the center or inside or outside of the border's outlines. There is only one option for the available shapes and that is a center outline.

Another exciting feature about the border is that we can customize the frame. You will find the setting icon next to the border's title. It has a dashed ends, caps, and arrows border. There are different ways to outline border such as the following:

1. There are three types of borders available for the line and the open paths. They are round cap, butt cap, and projecting cap. The butt cap lets you draw border-right to the vector point. The round cap lets you create a rounded, semi-circular end to a path that exists beyond the vector point. The last projecting cap enables you to create straight edges.

2. For three or more points and the path is closed and open. There are another three types of join. They are Miter join, Round join, and Bevel join. Miter join lets you create an angled join. Round join enables you to create a rounded corner, and the border-radius should be relative to border thickness. The last one, Bevel join, lets you create a chamfered edge on the border corner.

3. You can select the arrowhead for the start and end of the path in case of the line layers. You can switch the ends by choosing the **Layer > Path > Reverse Order**.

4. You can enter the value of the dash field to set the length of the dashes while creating dashed lines. The distances between the dashes automatically match using **Gap** fields; applying the condition, you don't set it to something different. You need to delete anything in the field if you wish to reset the **Gap** value and change it once again.

You can set the end type to the round type if you wish to create a dotted line, then you can fix the dash value to zero. The appearance of the dotted border changes if you will change the gap distance.

SHADOWS

Shadows and inner shadows work in different ways, although they have the same control. The basic difference between the shadow and inner shadow is that shadow renders outside the Layer, whereas in the case of inner shadow, the rendering is inside the Layer.

It is possible to apply multiple shadows to the same Layer and control their blending modes, color, blur radius, and X and Y positions.

You can click on the inner shadow + icon, blur + icon in the Inspector menu. You can adjust their values from there.

Shadows with blur values will not show on the Canvas when you zoom beyond 400%. It is interesting to note that the documents which use more shadows render quickly. Exporting any assets is not affected by this.

BLURS

Now we will understand some of the aspects of a blur. You need to click on the blur option in the Inspector to add blur to the Layer. There you will find a drop-down menu from which you can choose a blur type:

1. **Gaussian Blur:** It lets you apply a blur in all directions. You can use a slider to set the blur amount.

2. **Motion Blur:** It lets you apply blur in only one direction. This is basically to imply motion. Here, you can use the slider to set the blur amount and angle.

3. **Zoom Blur:** It lets you blur from one point outward. In this case, it is easy to set the blur amount and the point from where the blur starts.

4. **Background Blur:** It lets you replicate the blurs behind the overlays and panes in macOS. It enables you to set the content saturation. Here, the content which is underneath the Layer will become a blur. You can use the Inspector to develop the content saturation and blur amount. The fill style in this Layer, if any, needs to be transparent so that you can see the blur. Using the transparent fill, it's easy to tint it.

There are also some limitations with the blur. Applying much blur will slow down the mac app as it takes too much memory and processing power to render them.

TEXT STYLES

The best part about the Text Styles is that you can store a set of styles and reuse them across different text layers in the design you are working on. You can choose to update the text styles themselves so that each Layer that is using the text styles gets updated. You don't need to update Layer each time; instead, edit the text styles, and it will update all the Layer which is using the same text style.

You will see how to create a text style. First of all, you need to select the Layer and then choose the **Layer > Create new Text Style** from the menu. You can alternatively go to the Appearance panel in the Inspector and click on the **Create** + icon, which reads specifically No Text Style. You can give a name to your text style and then save it with the same.

Text style can also be created by using the Component View. You need to select the Text Style tab and then click on the + or **Create Text Style**. You can also edit the properties from the Inspector menu.

The next concept we will be learning is how to apply a text style. You will need to follow the steps:

1. Choose the pop-up menu that reads No Text Style after selecting a layer in the appearance panel in the Inspector.

2. You need to select the text style you want to apply in the component popover.

3. You can find the Style using the search bar. It appears at the top of the popover.

Alternatively, you can also apply text style using the Insert window. You need to choose the **Window > Insert** after pressing C. You can select or search the text style in the text style tab. You can create a new text layer by dragging and dropping it in the Canvas. You can apply the text layer by the drag and drop method.

Alternatively, you can use the Component View to apply a text style. You just need to select the text style and choose the **Insert Text with Style** from the Inspector.

The next thing we are going to learn is how to edit a text style? First of all, you need to make sure that you apply the text style which is to be edited. Select that Style and adjust the changes. You will find an asterisk appearing next to the text style's name after you are done with the editing. You have to choose any of the buttons in the Appearance panel in the Inspector from the following:

- **Update:** It lets you apply the adjustments to the Layer or any other layer.

- **Create:** It lets you create a new style with the update you made.

- **Detach:** It lets you keep the changes but remove the text style.

- **More:** It lets you rename a style or reset it.

The following method to edit text style is by using the Components View. You first need to switch to the Component View and then select the text style in the toolbar. You can make changes in the Inspector by choosing the Style you want to edit. This will make apply any changes to all layers automatically. You can share the text style by adding it to the library.

LAYER STYLE

It is very similar to the Text style. The fundamental difference is that they work with the shape layers while the text style works with the text layers. If you want to create a layer style, select the shape layer. You need to choose the **Layer > Create new Layer Style** from the menu. There is an alternate way to do this, and that is by using the Component View. You can choose the **Create Layer Style**. You can also create layer style from the library. There are library styles available for more details on this.

You can insert a text or layer style as a new layer via the insert window. For opening the insert window, you need to press the C button, and then you need to choose the **Window > Insert** in the insert menu +. You can find the Style which you wish to apply and then drag and drop in the Canvas. This will let you add text or layer style.

You can also use the Component window to insert a new text or layer style. For that, you need to switch to the Component mode first and then choose the component you want to insert. Finally, you need to click on the **Insert Shape with Style** or **Insert Text with Style**. This all process takes place in the Inspector. Alternatively, you can choose the insert menu from the toolbar, and from there, you can insert the text or layer style.

Organizing Style

In this section, we will learn how to create a group style in the component view and insert menu +. You can use the format **Group-name/Style-name**. For example, if you want to show a group background, then you can give it a name like a Background/light and Background/dark.

You can organize the Style in the component view. There are different things such as text style, layer style, and color variable, which can be contained in the Component View. It would be best if you held ⇧ for grouping several styles together. You have to choose all the styles you want to group. You can do this by control-clicking on any of the styles and then select the group. The new group appears in the left sidebar, and if you want to name the new group, you can do so by double-clicking on the new group and then name it.

For naming a specific style in the Inspector, you need to select the Style and then give that Style a name. Similarly, to rename an entire group that appears in the left sidebar, you can do it from there.

CONCLUSION

In this chapter, we learned the basics concepts of layers and how to work with them. We had seen how to select and group layers. We have learned grid making. We have learnt various techniques in aligning and resizing layers. We have learned smart distribution, moving layers, resizing Layers, etc.

CHAPTER 4

Vector Editing in Sketch

IN THIS CHAPTER

➤ Getting introduced to Vector Editing in Sketch

➤ We will look at drawing and editing Shape

➤ Understand working with points

➤ Learn opening and closing path

In the previous chapter, we dealt with the basic concept of layers and related operations on it. We learned how to select and group layers. We had gone through how to select multiple layers and how to select the overlapping layers. We had understood how to make grids. Then, we discussed how to align multiple layers, smart distribution features, and finally, we had seen resizing of layers.

DOI: 10.1201/9781003261575-4

In this chapter, we aim to learn the basics of Vector Editing in Sketch. We will see drawing and editing Shapes in Sketch. We will explore working with points. We will also focus on opening and closing paths.

DRAWING AND EDITING SHAPES

You can draw shapes using Vector tools, and for this, you need to click on **Insert > Vector** from the Toolbar. Alternatively, you can press V also.

First of all, you need to create two points by clicking anywhere on Canvas. The line that connects all points will give you a path, also called a segment. There is no limit to creating points but just connect with the first point again to choose a path. You create a mirrored path and curved path by clicking on the handle connecting points.

For editing shapes, you need to double-click on the shape layer. It is also possible to select multiple shapes and edit them at the same time.

WORKING WITH POINTS

Selecting Points

In editing mode, you can click and select any point. You can press the tab if you want to jump from one point to another or press the shift+tab to jump to the previous point.

By holding the upper arrow ⇧ and clicking on each LayerLayer, you can select multiple layers. To deselect, you need to click on the already selected point.

You can also select the inside point by just clicking and dragging on the outside points, and deselecting happens in the same manner. You can also select multiple points by clicking and dragging the method. For this, you need to enable the selection button next to X or Y points.

Alternatively, you can press ⌘+A to select multiple points.

How to Move Points?

You can change X and Y values in the Inspector bar by just selecting and dragging the point. Distribute and align tools are often used to distribute equally or align multiple points. We have already seen in the previous chapter how to use the Smart Distribution and alignment process.

Change Points Types

There are four different point types available to change the path in the Inspector bar. These are the following:

1. **Straight:** It gives you a straightforward path without any handle control point by default. For making a rounded corner on a straight point, you need to drag the radius slider. It is also possible to set individual radii for every point.

2. **Mirrored:** They create curved paths. They also provide two handle control points. You can drag any point, and another point will mirror it. You can also create mirror points by clicking and dragging while using Vector tools. It can also be done by double-clicking on any existing straight point.

3. **Disconnected:** They are entirely independent of each other. You can select any handle and press the

backspace button to delete that. This will make your curve a straight line. Alternatively, you can also do this by holding Ctrl while you drag its control handle. When you create a new point after a mirrored point, then that will be disconnected.

4. **Asymmetric:** They have different distances from the Vector point but contain a standard angle. To change the space from the Vector point, you need to hold ⇧ it while dragging the handle control point. This will not change the angle.

Alternatively, you can change the point type by pressing the following:

1 for the Straight

2 for the Mirrored

3 for the Disconnected

4 for the Asymmetric

How to Insert Points

A new point could be created between any points by hovering on the path and clicking on it. You can create a curve by holding and dragging the points. A new point will be made between the original path.

Bending a Segment

You need to press the Ctrl key and drag the segment to make a curve or bend. This will also create handle points to points on either side of it.

OPENING AND CLOSING PATHS

We have seen how to create a path between the points in the previous section. A Shape's path is generally closed or open in nature. If the path connects the first and last point, it is shut; otherwise, it is said to be open. There is a gap between the available paths.

You can create the relative path by choosing the **LayerLayer > Path > Close path** in the Menu. Alternatively, you can also press ⌘ + ⌥ + O. You can also open a path by this method.

It is easy to create an open path, and you need to add a point to your path and click on the **Finish Editing** in the Inspector. Next time when you work on the editing point, you need to place your next point after the last point or before the first point.

Scissor tools are also used to cut a path and make it open.

When working on the open path, if you click on the opposite points, then you can choose to close the path or select that point in preference.

The fill to an open path act like fill as if the path was closed.

How to Join a Path?

It can be done by choosing the **LayerLayer > Path > Join** from the Menu and combining them in one path. Except for the bottom path, other paths adjust their position slightly to fit together.

How to Point Snap a Pixel?

In the drop-down menu of the Inspector bar, you get the option to choose to snap to full pixel edges, half pixels, and not round at all needed.

To get a more precise idea about snapping pixels, enable pixel grid view. You can do this by choosing the **View > Canvas > Show pixel grid on Zoom**.

Zooming in will show all different pixel configurations.

Turn a Border into Outline

For turning a border into an outline, you need to choose **LayerLayer > Convert to Outline**. This will turn that border into an outline, and it has its own fill.

How to Offset Path?

For offsetting a path, you need to choose **LayerLayer > Path > Offset.** Doing this lets you contract or expand shapes. You can see the preview in the Inspector while you drag the slider in the Canvas. An Outline is also visible, which helps you compare with the original Shape. You can also make a duplicate layer. You can also add an offset path in the Toolbar by customizing the Toolbar. You need to choose the **View > Customize Toolbar**. You can drag the offset path to the Toolbar.

How to Reverse the Order of a Path?

In an open path Shape, you have a clear direction from start to end point. You can also reverse the direction by choosing the **LayerLayer > Path > Reverse Order** from the Menu. New points can be added at the opposite ends, and you can also reverse the direction of the arrow that is part of the border.

SHAPES

It is considered to be one of the most common layers of Sketch. It lets you add or edit premade shapes. It also enables you to create your own shapes using the vector tool.

Add Premade Shapes

You need to choose the insert button+ in the Toolbar in order to add a new shape. You can also use the insert menu in the menu bar. You need to choose the shape option and then select the type of shapes you want to add. You can add some premade shapes by using the following keys:

R: It lets you add a rectangle shape.

O: It lets you add oval shapes.

U: You can add a rounded rectangle.

L: It lets you add a line.

You can add the Shape just by clicking and dragging anywhere on the Canvas or the Artboard. As you drag, you will find the dimension of the Shape next to the cursor. You can make your Shape's height and width equal by holding the ⇧ while clicking and dragging. You can draw shapes from the center instead of the top left by just holding and dragging the ⌥. You can also change Shape's origin opposite to its size by holding the space bar as we click and drag. It is helpful, especially when you started at the wrong place.

Add Shapes with Pencil Tools

You can go to the Insert + Menu and choose the pencil tool in order to enable the pencil tool. Alternatively, you can also press P in order to do the same. You can draw the shapes which you like from there. The mac app smooths the curve after you are done with the drawing part. It also simplifies the path.

You can add shapes from the SVG code by just copying and pasting SVG code anywhere in the Canvas.

Edit Shapes in the Inspector

You will find the points for editing when you select a shape. You will find the points in the Inspector. There is a star icon. It basically lets you adjust the radius and the number of points.

You can adjust the corner radius by clicking on the rounded rectangle and then adjusting the radius in the Inspector. You can choose from two options, and they are round and smooth corners. It changes the way layers are drawn. You can create Squircles, the Shape used by the apple in their interface, using smooth corners. It also has curvature continuity. You can adjust the individual corner radius by choosing the personal corner point in the vector editing mode.

You can use two buttons in the Inspector bar to flip the shapes vertically or horizontally. The button remains selected (it lets you reverse again) until you make the surface flat and commit changes by choosing the **LayerLayer > Combine > Flatten**.

You can rotate shapes in the mac app. It lets you add values in degree in the Inspector. You can turn in the clockwise or counterclockwise direction by giving the positive or negative value in the degree. You can also use rotate button after selecting the shapes for rotating the shapes. You can turn the Shape by clicking and dragging anywhere outside the shapes.

You can click and drag the crosshair at its center to the point you want to rotate in order to change the axis on which your shapes rotate. You can reselect the Shape to reset it. You can hold ⌘ and drag any of its handles to rotate any shapes quickly. You can rotate the shapes in 15 deg increments by just holding the ⇧ while rotating a shape. You can reset the rotation value to 0 by flattening the shapes. You can choose to flatten the shapes by selecting the **LayerLayer > Combine > Flatten**.

Editing Shapes in Vector Editing Mode

You can edit a shape in vector editing mode by double-clicking on it or selecting it and pressing the enter key. You will find circular points connected by a path when you switch to the vector editing mode. You can change the Shape of any layer by clicking on any of the circular points and dragging them. You can insert a new point by just hovering between the points and clicking to insert. You can delete a point by just selecting it and pressing the backspace key. It all depends on the types of points connecting the path. The shapes may be straight lines or curves when you join the path between two points. You can change a path to curve ones by double-clicking on the points which connect the path. You will have the option to use two handle points when you change a point to create a curved path. You can also edit the curve itself. You can flatten your shapes by just choosing the **LayerLayer > Combine > Flatten**. It will let you create points at each end of the curve. You can go to the vector editing section if you want the details about it.

Editing Shapes using the Transform Tool

You can select one or more shapes to use the Transform tool. You can go to **LayerLayer > Transform > Transform**. Alternatively, you can also press the ⌘ + ⇧ + T in order to use the transform tool. You can also use the customized Toolbar to add the transform tool by choosing the **View > Customize Toolbar**. It lets you add points between each corner as well as add points to each LayerLayer of the shapes. You can skew the shapes by clicking on a point and dragging it. You can move both corners at the same time by clicking and dragging a point between two corners. You can control a single corner by holding the ⌘ key. The opposite corner move in the opposite direction when you click and drag a corner point. Scissor tool is used to edit shapes. It lets you cut away paths from a shape. You can enable the scissor tool by choosing the **LayerLayer > Path > Scissor**. The Toolbar can be customized by choosing the **View > Customize Toolbar**. You can also remove the Shape by clicking on any of the paths. So when you are done, click outside the Shape or press Enter key.

Rotate Copies Tool

You can edit the shapes using the rotate copies tool. You can rotate copies of a single shape around a single point. You can choose the **LayerLayer > Path > Rotate Copies**. You can also customize it and add a button to it for your Toolbar. You can select the number of copies you want to create and then press the ok button. This will make copies of the Shape. You can also set the position to your copies by using the handle that appears there. You can press Enter when you are done with that. Rotate copies will make the compound shape of the copies similar to the Boolean operation in mac app version 53.1 or earlier. You can choose **LayerLayer > Combine > Break apart** to turn this into a separate layer.

BOOLEAN OPERATION

You can combine and create complex shapes using four Boolean operations. You can click on the Boolean operation by selecting two or more shapes. You can do this in the Toolbar. These four operations are following:

- **Union:** It lets you create a shape that sums up multiple shape areas.

- **Subtract:** It enables you to remove the Shape's location from the one which is below it.

- **Intersect:** It lets you create a shape from the regions where selected shapes overlap.

- **Difference:** It lets you create a shape from the area where the selected shapes do not overlap. It is opposite to the intersect.

Touch bar lets you access the Boolean operations. Boolean operation work on the method of the top LayerLayer down. If you would like to create a donut shape and if you want to draw a smaller circle inside a larger circle, then apply the subtract operations.

The Boolean operation groups the original shapes into a single shape when you apply a Boolean operation to two or more shapes. It lets you create a new combined shape group. Boolean operations are nondestructive in a combined shape. You can use original shapes and edit them at any time. You can even use a new Boolean function to bring two or more combined shapes.

You can combine shapes in the layer list. It is possible to expand the combined Shape as you do with the regular groups in the layer list. You can find all the different shapes that made the combined shapes and the various Boolean operations. You can change the Boolean process that is applied to the LayerLayer by clicking on the Boolean operation icon next to the Shape. You can control-click on any layer in the layer list to hide any original shapes in your combined shapes. You can choose the **Hide Layer** option, and alternatively, you can press the ⌘ + ⇧ + H button. It will let you change the appearance of the combined shapes in the Canvas. You can also drag one Shape to the top of another shape in order to create the combined Shape in the layer list. This works on the principle of union Boolean operations.

MASKING SHAPES

You can create a mask in the shapes through different options in the mac app. You can use the lowest Shape in the layer list as a mask. You can also create an Outline mask. It will show all the multiple layers or parts of it that are within the Shape. You can also make them by a few methods. You need to choose the Canvas and then choose the **LayerLayer > Mask > Use a Mask**. You can also select a mask by control-clicking on the Shape. There will be the addition of icons when you create a mask to any layer above it in the layer list to show that they are being affected by the Mask. Any other layers or group which is dragged above it will also be affected by it. You can choose **LayerLayer > Mask > Ignore the underlying Mask** if you want to place objects above your Mask, and you do not like them to be included in the Mask. When you mask a group layer or a masked layer, then anything outside that masked LayerLayer won't be affected by it. You can mask multiple layers by selecting them at one time and then choosing the **LayerLayer > Mask > Mask with the Selected Shape**. The bottom list within the selection is used, and it will automatically group them all. You can control-click on the multiple layers selected and choose Mask, and that will have the same effect as the **Mask with Selected Shapes**. If you want to keep a mask layer within the group, then you can select a layer within the group and choose **LayerLayer > Mask > Ignore Underlying Mask**. The LayerLayer will remain within the group, but it won't be affected by it anymore.

Alpha Mask

It lets us hide anything that falls outside the shape layer in the mac app and allows us to adjust the opacity of the LayerLayer we are masking. You need to create a standard outline mask in order to create an alpha mask, and then you need to choose the **LayerLayer > Mask > Mask Mode > Alpha Mask**. This will make the alpha mask. You can take the gradient fill after you go to the Mask's LayerLayer fills in the Inspector. The mac app already filters the alpha in the gradient and not the color to control the mask settings. Shapes play an essential role in Sketch, and they are based on the Vector. They are also flexible.

LIBRARY

They contain Sketch components such as Symbols, Text, Styles, Color Variables, and layer styles. You can share them with the whole team. Document gets update notification if you update the components in the Library. You will be able to use the most updated components in your work, and you can review the changes. They are helpful when we are dealing with the components such as icons and UI elements. You can easily insert standard components such as Apple's iOS UI elements, and one of the best things about them is that they are constantly updated.

How to Create a Library

It is straightforward to turn a regular document into the Library. You can create a library in the mac app. You need to open the workspace or local document and then choose the **File > add as Library**. This will turn the documents into the Library and will add them to the Library. Similarly, you can also create a library in the web app. You can hover over the document's thumbnail, click on the cog icon, and then select the **Settings**. You can turn the workspace into the Library by enabling the **Share Symbols, Styles, and Color Variable**. In this way, you can mark your document as the Library, and everyone there can see that. You need to go to the library preference tab in the preference window in order to install the Library in the mac app. You can select the Library from there and then choose to install it.

You can add a library in the mac very conveniently. You can choose **Sketch > Preference** to open the preference window. You can also select the Ctrl+ to enable it. After that, click on the library tab. You can drag the document which is to be used as a library, and there is also the option to add a library. Similarly, you can add install a library from a web app. You need to go to the button right side of the document's sidebar in order to add a third-party library from the web app. You need to click on the **Add Library to Sketch**. If the Library is in the workspace and you choose to add a library, it will automatically add the Library to the mac app. In my Draft folder, the Library is available just for you. These are not useful to the whole team. One of the most valuable benefits of this is, you don't add unnecessary libraries to the team.

How to Share a Library?

There are various ways in which you can share the libraries. Some of them are sharing via your workspace, uploading to a server, using RSS for updates, and using a sync feature. The easiest of all is sharing via workspace. You just need to upload the document to the workspace and then open the setting. You can see the library section to check used as **Share Symbol, Style, and Color Variable**. You need to make the changes saved. You can find in the library tab in preference all of the workspace libraries for any team. You just go back to the mac app, and you will find it there. You can find a bundle of libraries there, and you need to choose which libraries you want to use and just install them from there. You can also share libraries by using the sync services such as Dropbox, Drive, etc. You just need to update it there and share it with other people. The person at the other end needs to add a library in the mac app. They get informed via notification if you make any changes or updates any. You can also share libraries using RSS and a server, but they are a bit more complex. They require hosting the libraries on the server, and then you need to create an XML file. You need to provide the following information inside the XML file:

- **<title>**: You have to provide a library name which you can show in the Sketch

- **<image><url>**: You will need to give the default thumbnail that Sketch is using in the Library. It shall be publicly accessible.

- **<item>**: You have to deliver what you want to create a new version of the Library. There is a need for one item tag within the feed. you need to include in the item tag:

  - **<pubDate>**: You have to provide the format in which the Library was updated.

  - You will get three attributes in the enclosure tag. They are URL, type, sparkle. You need to point to the server's location in the URL tag. You need to use HTTPS URLs to serve both the XML feed and Sketch file. You can encode your XML feed by using the Meyerweb URL encoder. You can open the full URL in a browser or in the mac app.

How to Rename a Library

You can follow these steps in order to rename your Library:

1. You need to choose **Sketch > Preference** to open the preference window. Alternatively, you can also press the ⌘ + to open that. Then, go to the library tab.

2. You can right-click on the Library, which is to be renamed, and then choose rename.

3. You can use Finder to rename the Library.

4. You can add Library again.

Library Symbols

You can use the insert window or insert + menu to browse and insert library symbols. You can open the insert window by pressing the C button. You can also choose the **Window > Insert** from the menu bar. You can go to the left-side bar and find the libraries there. The search bar is used to search for symbols. You can add the symbols to the Canvas by the drag and drop method. You may also use the insert + menu to access the library symbols icon. You can also find the library symbols in the Inspector.

Edit Library Symbols

You can edit library symbols by double-clicking on them, and you can find the location from which the Library has been added. You can double click on the Symbol to edit in the local Library, and you will have the following options:

5. **Open in Library:** You will have the option to go to the original library document to edit the Symbol's source. It will use instances of that Symbol to update the Library and any documents.

6. **Unlink from Library:** It will help in creating a local version of the Symbol. You can go to the current document and edit its source. Doing this, you will not be able to see the updates to that Symbol if its original Library gets updated.

You will see the following options if you are trying to edit a symbol that's part of the Library:

7. **Open in Library:** It will go to the shared workspace and open the original Library documents. The update made here will be the update for the whole team. The document with that Symbol's instances will show changes.

8. **Unlink from Library:** It will create a local version of the Symbol where you can edit its source from the current document. You will no longer get the update from the Symbol if any update is made to its original Library.

You have to take extra care if you use the Library as a part of a team while editing symbols. Everyone using that Library will get the updates or any changes made. Anyone with the starred update can see the changes to that Library if you mark star to library updates. Unstarred updates do not go automatically if changes are made or updated to the user. You get only the option to unlink from the Library if the Symbol you want to edit belongs to a third-party library like the Apple iOS UI kit.

Library Styles

Besides symbols, you can also use Libraries to sync and share text and layer styles. You will get them under the appearance section in the Inspector, and they will appear in the insert window and in the component popover. One can also use the Insert menu to access text and layer styles. To indicate that they are part of the Library, they have a link next to their group name. You can press C to insert a library from the Insert window, or you can choose **Window > Insert** from the menu bar. You can go to the left-side bar and find all of the enabled libraries. You can filter results or search for text style by clicking on the libraries. You can simply drag them to the Canvas.

Edit Library Styles
If you are working with library styles and if you wish to edit that, then you will find some useful options in the Inspector menu:

9. It would be best to create a new local style from the currently selected style before you make any edits. Users will create a unique library-style in your document by unlinking style from the Library.

10. You can unlink it from the Library by detaching the style from its source.

11. You can choose to create a new style and replace it to unlink it from the Library. You can apply those changes to every layer, and you can also choose to reset style to revert the changes.

12. You can choose edit style in the Library as long as the style is not part of a third-party library.

Anyone will get the update if the editing is done to the Library.

Creating Library Presets
You can use libraries to create presets. You can sync or share the gradient or image fills presets. You can create Library presets from the image fill. You can select the gradient in

the fill popover of library documents, and then you can add it as presets under the Document Colors. You can use color variables to create, share, and sync solid colors in your libraries. You can view all of the available Library presets when you are working on a document that uses the Library. One needs to click on the title above presets in the fill popover.

How to Update Library Components?

You will find library update notifications when the library components (symbols, text styles, color variables, or layer styles) get updated. The components updates dialogue box appears if you click on this. You can select the component to see what has changed and check the checkbox if you want to update it. You can uncheck if you don't want to update specific components. You can find the most recent Library updates when you change a component in the Library and save a new update. You can click on the library update available notification in the preference window and download it. You can stop updating a symbol by double-clicking on it and clinking on the unlink from the Library. You can also create a custom library thumbnail.

CONCLUSION

In this chapter, we had a brief introduction to Vector Editing in Sketch. We learned drawing and editing Shapes. We had understood working with the points and introduced to selecting, moving, changing points, etc. We learned the techniques of opening and closing paths. We learned to join a path. We had learned various other methods, such as turning the border into an Outline and offset path.

CHAPTER 5

Understanding the Sketch App

IN THIS CHAPTER

> ➤ To acquire knowledge about Images and Data in Sketch

> ➤ To explore various functions like Insert, reduce, and replace images

> ➤ We will also see Bitmap image editing, color popover, and image fills

> ➤ Understand working with the data and linked data

> ➤ Learn about the Text

> ➤ Learn about the Symbols in the Sketch

In the previous chapter, we saw Vector Editing in Sketch. We learned the concept of drawing and editing in Sketch.

DOI: 10.1201/9781003261575-5

We understood working with the points. We had learned various other concepts such as selecting, moving, and changing points.

We also saw inserting a new point and bending the path. We learned the concepts of opening and closing paths. We saw how to join a path, how to snap a pixel, how to turn a border into an Outline, and how to reverse the order of the path.

In this chapter, we will understand the Sketch app in a more contextual manner. We will learn about images and data in the Sketch app. We will learn about Text and Symbols in Sketch in a more detailed way.

IMAGES AND DATA

In this section, we will see how to add image fills and images from data sources. It will be done in the existing layers. It is possible to add regular Bitmap images into Sketch documents.

How to Insert Images?

You can insert images in the document by simply dragging it from the desktop or by searching it and dragging it from the search bar. Alternatively, you can also choose to insert images by choosing **Insert > Images.**

How to Replace Images?

Suppose you have done the resizing and styling of an image in your document, and if you want to replace the image for any reason, you can do this by selecting the images and choosing **Layer > Image > Replace.** This way, your image will be replaced. It is one of the most delicate features in the Sketch app, which designers frequently use to suit their needs.

How to Reduce Image Size?

If you keep adding a lot of images in your document, then your file size will increase, which will lead to a slowdown of the App and also alter its efficiency. No designer would like his App to work in an inefficient manner, so to counter this problem, you need to reduce the size of the image. You can do this by choosing **Layer > Image > Minimize File Size**. The file size will be reduced by changing the image resolution.

How to Edit Bitmap Images?

The Sketch app consists of a small section of Bitmap Editing tools. In order to use them, you need to select the image on the Canvas and then double-click on that image, which will enter into editing mode. There are two tools in the Inspector which you can use:

1. **Selection:** It lets you select the rectangular area on the image.

2. **Magic Wand:** You can use this to click and drag on the image to select a specific area. The more the drag, the greater the selection tolerance.

Further, you can add and subtract further Selection to your Selection. To add additional Selection to your existing Selections, you just need to hold ⇧ the key, and a new Selection will be added to the Current Selection.

Similarly, to subtract a Selection from your existing Selections, you need to hold ⌥, and this will subtract a Selection from the Existing Selection. The other tools which you can use are

1. **Invert:** It lets you flip your Selection. Doing this makes the Unselected area a Selected area.

2. **Crop:** It lets you crop the Layer to include the Selection.

3. **Fill:** It lets you fill a Selection with a color from the color popover.

After you have finished editing, you need to click outside the image or press Esc or Enter.

Color Adjust Panel in the Inspector lets you make basic, nondestructive color adjustments to the image. To do this, you need to select the image you want to edit, then move the slider to adjust the hue, brightness, saturation, and contrast.

Image Fills

The Sketch app supports various image files such as:

1. Image fill.

2. Angular Gradient.

3. Solid Fill.

4. Linear Gradient.

5. Radial Gradient.

You should know that by default, all new layers have single, solid color fills.

To add a new fill, you need to click on the + button in the fill panel. It is possible to add as many fills as one wishes to add. The additional fills will stack on top of each other. Following options are available for each fills created:

1. **Opacity:** Besides blending modes, one can also change fill's opacity to collaborate and show two or more fill types.

2. There is also a method to enable/disable the Checkbox.

3. **Color Swatch:** You can click on the Color Swatch icon and navigate through all the available Color Variables in the libraries and the documents.

4. **Color/Preview Well:** It lets you select a different color or change the fills type. We will see in detail about Color popover later on.

5. **Blending Mode:** It lets you select a blending mode by clicking on the icon. If selected anything other than usual, then it will change the icon's color to blue.

6. **Fill Options:** Color HEX value is available if you are going to use a solid color fill. You can do the copy/ paste from here. There will be an option to change the types if you are using a gradient or image fill. The alpha value set for the color will preserve if you change the hex value of a color in the color picker.

You can press the F button, and it will toggle the visibility of all fills of the selected Layer.

To add an image file, you need to click on the fill's options and then check the image fill button, which appears on the right side of the popover. From there, you can select your own image from **Choose Image.** You can also pick the image from the preset, which appears at the bottom of the popover. You can also select from the data source by clicking on the data icon.

Following are the four different types of fills from which you choose:

1. **Fit:** It lets you adjust the size of the image in order to adjust to the Layer's height.

2. **Fill:** It lets you adjust the size of the image to adjust to Layer's width.

3. **Stretch:** It lets you stretch the image and fill the height and width to fit the image.

4. **Tile:** It lets you keep the image in the original size and also option to adjust it.

You can also see frequently used documents from the clock icon above the image preview. You can also choose a basic pattern or noise fill from the global presets at the bottom.

For the Overlapping path, you can change the fill setting. After you have applied fill to a shape, click on the setting icon, which appears near the fills section title. You can choose the non-zero or odd-even rule to fill the shape. Shapes are filled according to the **winding rule**.

It is a method to determine whether a point falls within an enclosed curve or not. It is used in two-dimensional graphics. The winding rule counts the number of revolutions counterclockwise around the point without doubling back on itself.

The Color Popover

Color well is used to fill, show border, or shadow. The Color Popover consist of the following:

1. **The fill icons:** It lets you switch between the solid, gradient, and image fills. It let you change the color popover's setting to match.

2. **The text field:** It provides you access to the HEX value of a color, and you can use this in copy/paste. You can also set color manually by RGB and alpha values. It lets you switch between Hue, Saturation, Brightness (HSB) or Hue, Saturation, lightness (HSL).

3. **The color picker:** Here, Hue, Saturation, Brightness (HSB) model is used. You can change the color saturation by dragging from left to right and adjust the brightness by dragging the point from up to down.

4. **The sliders:** It controls alpha(opacity) and color's hue.

5. **The preview:** It lets you know the final set of colors.

6. **The eyedropper:** You can pick any color from inside or outside of your display. It is accessible by selecting a layer and then pressing Ctrl + C button.

Data Tool

Data tool plays a significant role when you need to add different Text and images to your document and create realistic prototypes. By default, there are several data sources in the Sketch app, but these can be split into three types:

1. **Text data:** It consists of real names and cities.

2. **Image data:** It includes a set of user's photos and tiles.

3. **Linked Data:** It consists of a collection of user-profiles which include pictures and a short bio.

More complex data sources can be from third-party Data plugins. By default, you can use the Unsplash plugin from which you can search and insert an image from its library.

Working with Data

If you want to add data to a layer or shape, select that Layer or shape and click on the data icon in the toolbar. Alternatively, you can choose **Layer > Data** and then choose the type of data you want to insert. You can see random data in the data source by default. You can check the random data from the data source by toggling the Insert data at the random Checkbox in the data menu.

To refresh or clear data, you need to press ⌘ + ⇧ + D or go to the Data menu and click on refresh data to fill the Layer with different images. You can click on the **Disconnect from Data Source** if you wish to remove a connection between a layer and your Data Source. Remember, it won't store your original data.

For using data with Symbols where designers can add multiple Data Sources to different layers in the Symbol, it also lets you refresh all at the same time. There is a Data icon next to each Symbol which you can use to refresh or add Data within a Symbol.

It lets you add your own data sources to the Data tab in preferences.

Data tab preferences have the following:

1. **Toggle visibility:** You can enable to Checkbox to make data sources visible. It is helpful when you have lots of data sources.

2. **Add data:** It lets you add data from anywhere on the computer, and you can add the data in the documents by drag and drop.

3. **Control clicking:** This will enable the option to show it in the finder by clicking on the data source. It also lets you remove it altogether.

4. **The menu:** It gives you information about the data sources which is selected.

Your data source shall be in a place that doesn't change. Don't move your data sources after you have added them. Otherwise, your Sketch won't be able to find it.

You can create your own text data source and save it as a text file, and the data value shall be on a new line:

Afghanistan

Albania

Algeria

...

You can create an image data source via data tab preference. For this, you need to create a folder containing all different images and add it via that data tab preference.

How to Work on Linked Data?

When you have Linked Data, you can use JSON files. It lets you helpfully combine different sets of data. It makes it easier to stress test your design.

You need JSON files that contain the Data you need. The format of the JSON file is:

```
[
{
"Photo": "mango.jpeg",
"Location": New Delhi, India",
"Title": "Avenue of the Baobabs",
"Trees": "60 trees",
},
{
"Photo": "Date.jpeg",
"Location": "Kabul, Afghanistan",
"Title": "Date Forest",
"Trees": "200 trees",
},
{
"Photo": "bamboo.jpeg",
"Location": "Assam, India",
"Title": "Assmo Bamboo Forest",
"Trees": "1500 trees",
}
]
```

Nested Data Structure is also used in JSON files and also in Symbols and groups. Here, you use the group name in the nested within each set of data.

```
[
{
"name": "Martin Luther",
"avatar": "/Faces/110.jpg",
"location": "Malaysia",
"bio": "Cricket lover, karate champion,
and traveler",
"social": {
"handle": "@MartinLuther01",
"bio": "Loving life and living in Texas"
}
},
]
```

You have to add JSON file as Data Source in the Preference window in the same manner as you would do with any other data source. You need to save images files on your App. Designers need to keep both JSON and image files together in a folder. Resizing images is preferable for better performance.

You can also use Linked Data in the existing design. For that, you need to name the JSON file in the same name as the layers in a group or Symbol in design. After that, choose the group or Symbol and then select the JSON data from the Data toolbar item. You can also do this via the contextual menu.

You will not be able to apply Linked Data from the Inspector if you select a group of layers or Symbols.

You can also use the Linked Data on the blank Canvas. Linked Data is also used to add a new set of layers to Canvas. For this, you need to choose data from the list and then select the Data which you want to use. The Linked Data can also be arranged as a grid to add more entries and choose refresh data to refresh each Layer with the updated information.

There is also an option to install Data Plugins just like regular plugins, and they will provide you the opportunity to use a range of data. You can build a Data Supplier Plugin for Sketch. If you bring the actual data into Sketch, you can test the design. Things can be taken further by creating a data plugin. Data was introduced as a new feature in Sketch 52. This feature lets you bring data into your design and also enables you to solve the typical use case. For complex needs, such as if your Data is entirely predictable rather than random, then? What if you need your data to be more innovative?

The data feature was designed in such a way that it was as simple as it could be. At the same time, space for advanced users was also provided. It let them expand the functionality. A new API was introduced to cater to the need, and that was **Data Supplier**. This enables you to add the Sketch Plugins, which allows you to add Data Sources to the App. The customers benefit from all the cool features of plugins. We will learn how to build a Data Supplier Plugin, but before that, we will explore how Data features works. It is worth knowing beforehand.

Two types of the Layer are supported by Sketch for layers: **images and plain Text**. You can add multiple data types with a single plugin, so it is possible to add both image and Text using a single plugin. So when anyone selects any layers in Sketch or clicks on the override data icon in the

Inspector, then Sketch enables relevant sources for all layer types. Later on, we will see the registration of plugins for each Data type. Suppose you want to access some data in the plugins, then it passes the request to relevant plugins, and there is also some important information provided in the context Data. The plugin tries to generate the data, gather it, or download it. At the same time, you can also send an array of data in a single step. It will return the Data one by one. That is dependent on the speed to download the data.

We will see the code that a data supplier plugin uses. It is easier for you to follow the lesson if you are familiar with JavaScript. The command-line tool is used to generate, develop, and publish Sketch Plugins, skpm. If that is not installed on the computer, then you need to run the following in the terminal.

```
npm install --global skpm
```

Skype generally requires Node.js to be installed beforehand, but we will not be discussing this here as it is beyond the scope of Sketch.

The best thing about the skpm is its ability to generate plugins. If you want to create a new plugin, then enter the following code:

```
Skype create datademo --template=skpm/
with-data supplier
```

It will create a datademo folder, and you need to add some files to it and download all the required dependencies. It would be best if you run the following:

```
cd data demo
```

And then, you need to run the following:

```
npm run build
```

The data plugin will be built in Sketch. It will appear in the new Data Section.

You can add a bunch of data to a new document, and then if you select the **Data > datademo**. It will help you see the sample plugin doing.

To understand what's going on in the code, open your code editor then you need to open the datademo folder. Open src/my-command.js, you need to ignore the function like *onStartup* and *onShutdown*. It would be best if you went directly to *on supply data* option. This is the way how Sketch works. It does four things at the time it asks for plugins:

1. It takes the data key from the context in order to return the Data later.

2. It operates over layers affected by the action.

3. A random number is generated for each one.

4. Data is sent back to Sketch.

The key attribute will get it from the context Data object. You will get a critical feature that will act as a UUID that a plugin uses to return the data.

The array contains the list of layers or overrides that Sketch needs.

```
let data key = context.data.key
```

For achieving the step 2 forEach will work on collection of layers. The collection is available at *context.data.item*. It all depends on how the user triggers the feature, the items become layer or overrides:

```
const items = util.toArray(context.data.
item).map(sketch.fromNative)
item.forEach(item,index)=>{
Write the stuff here.
}
```

Step 3 will generate the random number.

```
let data = Math.random().toString()
```

In the next step, you forward the data to the DataSupplier, sending it back to Sketch.

```
DataSupplier.supplydataAtIndex(data
key,data, index)
```

Here, datakey is passed to the (context.data.key). The Data is sent one by one using SupplyDataIndex, and the Data is stored at the index.

```
let count= context.data.items.count()
let datakey=context.data.key
let data = Array.from(Array(count)).map(i=>
Math.random().toString())
DataSupplier.supplydata(datakey,data)
```

It is similar to work with images. In the image file, you need to provide a path to the image.

Now, we will see how to register the plugin with Sketch. We already have code that has generated random numbers, but we need to let Sketch know about it. You need to add an attribute to manifest.json

```
"suppliesData": true
```

It is necessary to tell Sketch about the data types our plugins provide. We need to tell Sketch which functions to call in order to get Data from the plugin. Action section in the Manifest File is used to do this; handlers to Startup and Shutdown are added here. It is allowed to use any name, but here we are using SupplyData as an example.

```
{
"actions":{
"Startup": onStartup",
"Shutdown": "onShutdown",
"SupplyData": onSupplyData"
}
}
```

To register the Startup plugin.

```
export function onStartup(){
DataSupplier.registerDatasupplier('public.
text','datademo','SupplyData')
}
```

Doing this will register DataSupplier, which is datademo for SupplyData.

We will learn more about DataSupplier feature later on. This content was so rich in information, and I hope this would have added an updated knowledge to your collection.

Sketch 52 has provided the most significant updates with many new features. It reveals the future of Sketch designs. It has come up with dark mode, Style Overrides, new combined shapes, and a newly designed interface. Here are the followings updates:

1. It lets us use dark mode in macOS Mojave.

2. It has come up with an updated UI design.

3. It allows us to design with data and performs various other operations with data in Sketch.

4. There is a way to override the Text and Layer Styles in Symbols.

5. It has provided many updated enhancements.

Dark Mode has got a positive response from the designer across the world. It followed the plugins such as brilliant Midnight. Dark Mode was the choice among the designers. The announcement was made by Apple at Worldwide Developers Conference (WWDC) about the introduction of dark mode. It lets you focus on things of importance and ignore the unnecessary stuff. It is helpful primarily when you work at night or during the dark hours, and it provides comfort to the eyes. It has followed guidelines issued by Apple and comes with limited use of color and clear iconography. The Canvas will be white until you draw on Artboard. It is easy to see what you are working on.

The updated Sketch 52 supports Mojave's new Accent and also supports features like highlight color. The systemwide preference will be matched to the highlighted UI elements in Inspector, Layer List, and anywhere in the App.

It is linked to the system preference and activated accordingly on system-wide importance in Mojave. There will soon be an in-app preference that will be available in Sketch very more quickly. We will see the future look of Sketch. It has totally redesigned its interface. It has come up usability, legibility, and workflow in the mind. It also updated and came up with a clean, new Layer List, a new Inspector, and a new iconography.

A new filtering system is introduced as part of the Layer List redesigned. It is possible now to choose filter layers by type, which lets you view shapes, images, groups, and slices.

Keywords are used to filter layers. Sticky Artboard titles are included when you make changes to the layer list. It is now possible to tell where you are even when you are scrolling through endless layers. The Inspector also makes changes when we talk about the improved readability and workflow speeding up. The Inline Text and border settings are included in the Highlights. There is also an option to inline HEX value for solid fills, export preview available for exportable layers, and a new resizing preview.

There is the presence of a collapsible feature that shows you information that is needed. It has become easier to read and navigate through the documents more smoothly.

This version has come up with a totally redesigned toolbar with new icons and a new default order. It has become more convenient to customize the toolbar. It lets you access necessary features which are suitable for your design workflow. Sketch has improved its performance, and there are changes under the hood. It has become smoother to move, resize, and manipulate layers.

Now, you can design data at your fingertips. You can create with the data such as Text, images, and other data. Lorem ipsum is replaced by fundamental data. It is accessible easily. The images and Text are added from the mac folder with the help of data in Sketch. There is also an option to use plugins to generate all kinds of images and text data which you want to generate from any source. It allows you to use Text, images, and many more. Four data types are recently allowed to use – Names, Faces, World Cities, and tiles. There is an option to try the new Data menu in the toolbar. You can refresh the content of the data by pressing Command-Shift-D. You can create data layers inside symbols, and this will allow you to refresh multiple data sources. Therefore, you can easily create reusable UI elements and restore its entire content at once.

You will be able to add accurate data to your designs. It has made rapid prototyping quite a quicker process. Now, your creations can be more diverse and inclusive, and you can do this with the help of the data. Data sources are created by considering multiple diversity in mind, such as ethnic, cultural, or gender diversity.

For example, if we take Names and Faces, they are ethnically diverse with 50/50 gender diversity. This shows inclusivity. Apart from this, you can test your design by using various data sets. You can also test UX with names, places, and information.

We have come to know that possibilities in Sketch are endless with the ability to create Data plugins for Sketch. They are some brilliant features, such as translate your text content to another language. It is also collaborated with Unsplash to make the plugins, and these come with enhanced features such as adding royalty-free images from the library. A guide is available at the Developer blog for those who want to work with Data in Sketch.

This version also came up with the overrides to Text and Layer Styles, and that is inside Symbols. They are overridden, similar to the Text, images, and symbols. You can swap the style or Layer with another layer using the overriding features in Text Style. Things like text color can be easily changed with this feature, with the condition that you have defined similar Text Styles beforehand.

The Layer Style is also overridden in a similar manner. You need to choose the saved style from the Inspector.

Now, we are going to look at all new combined shapes. We know that Boolean operations are the most powerful tool that is available in Sketch. It is possible to create complex combined shapes, illustrations, and icons using Boolean operations. Nesting introduction and Boolean operation improvement are general in this updated version. You can use Union, Subtract, Intersect, and Difference tools according to the need. Complex shapes can be created by combining any number of shapes or symbols. The image can be complex. It has become relatively easier to work with really detailed icons or illustrations.

Sketch has come up with the improved Sketch Cloud. The improvements are independent of the App. Following are some of the recent changes:

1. It has improved the upload process and thus increased reliability.

2. It is easier to check who can see your document and share it using a redesigned share setting model.

3. You can describe the document in the new document sidebar. It made it easy to add a link to relevant sources.

4. It has come up with add library and download document button. These are not located in the header but instead moved to the sidebar.

5. Sketch Cloud is the best and the easiest way to share and upload Sketch documents. It has interactive prototypes.

TEXT

For adding or inserting a text, select **Insert > Text** from the menu bar or toolbar. Alternatively, you can press T and start typing anywhere in the Canvas.

A fixed-sized textbox can be created using the click and drag feature. This will complete the fixed-sized textbox. You do not need to expand the size of the text box; but instead, the Text will wrap into new lines.

If you want to add Text from another app then, select the **Edit > Paste > Paste as rich Text**. Alternatively, you can press Ctrl + Alt + ⇧ + V. If you want to add Text to a vector path, then find a text layer and then select **Text > Text on** the way. Now, you can draw a text layer to shape the Layer and snap it into place.

To remove Text from the path, you need to do the same process again, and it will remove Text from the path.

The Inspector provides you to change the Text option, and you can change its appearance in the Text menu in the menu bar. It depends on the font. If it supports the open type feature, you will find them in the Text menu. You will find the Inspector if it has Variable options.

You can also change the Text using the text menu. If you will go to the Text menu bar, then you will find options for:

1. Kerning, ligature, and baseline.

2. Basic styling features such as bold, italic, underline.

3. You can increase/decrease alignment and size.

4. You can create ordered/unordered lists.

5. You can transform between uppercase and lowercase.

MacOS coordinating system points are used to measure all layers including Text. Here, one point is equivalent to one point on the Canvas. The question which arises to our mind is that, does Sketch measure in point or pixel?

So the answer to this question is: Sketch uses a macOS coordinate system. So everything including the Text layer is measured in points.

You will find the formatting option after you have selected the Layer. The properties will be visible in the Inspector section. You can save and apply the Text Styles in the appearance panel. It helps you keep the different Layer's appearance inconsistent with the design. We have already seen how to apply Text Style. It lets you select the text layer's typeface type, such as font size, color, and weight.

In case if you are using the Variable option OpenType font, then you need to click on the variable option button to reveal all the options under it. You can adjust the individual properties by adjusting the slider. Character, line, and paragraph are used to change the spacing between characters, lines, and paragraphs, respectively. There are also options such as Auto width, Auto Height, and fixed-width, which are used to resize to fit. Auto width lets you expand the width as much as possible in order to fit the Text in a single line. Only horizontal alignment is allowed in this case.

Auto Height lets you adjust the height to fit the height of the text box, and you can adjust the height of the textbox to adjust the content.

Fixed width lets you set the height and width of the Text. You can crop the Text if it exceeds the width else it will fit the width and height. Here, you can set both vertical as well as horizontal alignment.

You can use the alignment in the button to set the vertical and horizontal alignment of the Text.

You can click on the cog icon which appears on the top of the text panel in order to open the Text Options panel. Using this, you can do the following things:

1. You can use the features like underline and strikethrough.

2. You can transform the Text from the upper to lower or vice versa. They are nondestructive in nature; therefore, you can transform all to uppercase automatically.

You can also edit the multiple text layers at the same time. For this, you need to hold ⇧, and then you have to select the layers which you want to edit. You can adjust the styling of the Text by going to the Inspector and then the text menu. You can save your changes by clicking anywhere in the Canvas.

You can create and customize lists. You need to select a layer in order to create a list, and then you can go to **the Text > List Type** menu and select the bullet or number. It gives you option to customize the appearance of the list. You can highlight the list and prefixes, suffixes, or bullets. You can do this by choosing the **Text > List Type > List Options**.

You can select your Text and choose Text > OpenType Features on the condition that your font supports the OpenType features. You can enable OpenType features from the menu bar.

You can change the Text of the color. You can use a color button within the text panel to apply different colors to different parts of the layers. You can use the fills option in the fill panel, but this will affect the whole text layer and is considered ideal for applying the gradient. Any color which is set in the text panel will get overridden by this.

You can adjust line-height. Generally, line-height adjusts to match its font size when you create a new layer. It will reposition itself if you will manually adjust the line height, but the first baseline will always stay in place. The line height will remain consistent if you change the font-weight in the paragraph.

You can convert Text to vector shapes. For that, you have to select the first Layer and then choose **Layer > Convert to Outlines**. Applying Boolean operation will have the same effect as converting to outlines. You can edit the text layer. But it is a destructive process. It generally slows when you convert a lot of Text to outlines.

You can also manage fonts. You can manage them from the document setting window. You have to choose **File > document setting**. You will see a missing font when you have no embedded fonts in the top right of the window.

In case of missing font, you will see a pdf preview, but you will not be able to edit them. you can click on the missing fonts to replace them with missing fonts. This can be done by choosing the **File > Document setting**.

You can also embed fonts. It is very helpful when you share the document with other users and if they have not installed that font but you embedded that in yours. For this, you need to check the documents you uploaded display the text layers accurately.

This applies to nonsystem fonts and supports the most OpenType fonts.

You can do the embedding from the **Document Setting Window** via **File > Document Settings**.

SYMBOLS IN SKETCH

They speed up your workflow, you can save them and reuse them throughout your designs. Any changes made to Symbol made the change appear everywhere. For a specific part of the symbols, you can also create overrides.

Now, we will see how to create a Symbol. After selecting any Artboard, layers, or groups, you need to choose the **Create** icon in the toolbar, then **Layer > Create Symbol.** You can name your Symbol and then decide whether to send it to the source version or keep it on the same page on which you are working currently.

You create a source and an instance when you create a Symbol. You can have only one source, but you can create as many Symbols as you want. It will show to any of the instances in your documents if you make any changes to the source. you will get a new layer list above the source when you choose Symbols to send to the Symbol page. If you don't send it to the abovementioned, then it will appear in the Artboard.

You can create symbols back to a layer. For this, you need to select the Symbol's source in the layer list. You can choose **Layer > Convert Symbols to Artboard**. It will be applied to the group and no more instances. You can replace a layer with Symbols. You need to click on the Layer and then choose to **replace with** and then choose a symbol. It also fits the symbol size.

You can insert Symbols in three ways. These are the Insert Window, Component View, and Insert menu.

Insert a Symbol through Insert Window

You can press C to open the insert menu or choose **Window > Insert**. You can search for the Symbol which you are looking for and then drag and drop them into the Canvas.

The other way to insert a symbol is via the insert menu +. It is used to browse the Symbol or search the File quickly and search for what you are looking at. You can also insert Symbols via the Component View, and for that, you need to first switch to the Component View; you can do this from the top left of the toolbar to toggle between the Canvas and the Component View. All Symbols in the documents are visible. You can look for the Symbol in the top right of the Component View and find the Symbol you are looking for. You can click on the Insert in the Inspector once you find your Symbol.

How to Edit a Symbol?

You can edit a symbol in mainly two ways. Either you edit them as the override or content in the Symbol Source.

You can edit in the symbol source, but for that, you need to find your symbol source you can also go straight to it by double-clicking anywhere on it. The edit which you make to the source will apply to the design as they are synced. You can choose return to instances once you have made changes, and you can also check your progress.

The instances with overrides appear in the Inspector. You can change the content inside the individual symbol instances by editing the overrides in the Inspector. You don't need to alter any changes to the source.

You can hover over to the symbol highlight and then show it in the Inspector. This proves to be beneficial in case a lot of overrides is there or nested overrides.

You can also choose the specific override by clicking on the triangle next to the Symbol's name.

Specific actions like moving or duplicating will apply to the whole instances even if you have focused on the specific overrides. To change the override layer itself, you need to use the Symbol instances.

You can also use text overrides. You can change their contents. You can type it in new content by double-click on the Layer in a Symbol instance.

It will change to the Text in the symbol source if any-thing is deleted. You can populate the override by using the data icon.

Drag the image in the preview to override any image layer with fill in the Inspector and then choose the image. You can also use the Data icon to do the same. You can click on the image preview and if you want to remove the image then press the backspace.

You can find in the override panel in the Inspector if you have applied any text or layer Style to your design.

You can also override a prototyping hotspot. You can over-ride its target Artboard or you can choose None to disable it.

You can also show and hide overrides. In the manage override panel, there is a checkbox. You can choose which one to be available in the Symbol's instances. You can also rest overrides. For this, you need to select any instances and then press on the reset icon next to the override panel title. You can also detach a symbol instance from a symbol source. By detaching only, you can edit the individual instances.

You can do this by choosing the **Layer > Detach from Symbol**. You can also detach by control-click on the Symbol and then choose to detach from Symbol. Any nested group in the instances can also be detached.

You can swap symbols using component popover in the Inspector. You can search for the Symbol and swap it.

You can use the scale command to scale and resize Symbols. You can do this by choosing the **Layer > Transform > Scale**. It will not affect the source but the styles like border will decrease or increase in proportion.

CONCLUSION

In this chapter, we learned that how to insert, replace, and reduce images. Then we have seen editing of Bitmap images and then image fills in a detailed manner. We learned about color popover and data tools. We understood working with the data and also explored working with the Linked Data. We understood the concept of Text. At last, we learned about the Symbols in Sketch. We have seen how to insert a Symbol and edit a Symbol.

CHAPTER 6

Prototyping

IN THIS CHAPTER

➤ Acquiring fundamental knowledge about Prototyping

➤ Understanding the fundamentals of adding Links

➤ Understanding fundamentals of adding Hotspots

➤ Learning how to create fixed elements

➤ Techniques of previewing

In the previous chapter, we have understood about the Sketch app in a more detailed manner. We have seen how to insert images, replace images, and reduce the image size. We learned how to edit Bitmap images. We learned about image fills and color popover. We had hands-on experience in using the data tool. We understood working with data and especially the Linked data. We dealt with the concepts of the Text in the Sketch app. We learned about the

DOI: 10.1201/9781003261575-6

Symbols in Sketch. We learned about various operations, such as inserting a symbol or editing a symbol.

In this chapter, we are going to learn about Prototyping in Sketch. We will see the fundamentals of adding Links and adding Hotspots. We will learn how to create Fixed Elements, and at last, we will see previewing prototypes.

It is convenient to preview the designs and navigate through the design using Prototyping. You can navigate between the Artboards and animated interactions. We will be learning the applications of the Prototyping features such as Hotspots and start points. This feature gives life to the designs. You can find the Prototyping tutorial under the Templates tab in the Documents Window.

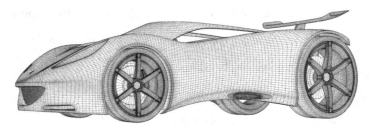

ADDING LINKS

You can create a link between the Artboards if you wish to create a Prototype. It is convenient to add Links from any layer to any Artboards.

You need to choose + next to Prototyping in the Inspector to add a link. Alternatively, you can also press the W for the same purpose. You have to click on the Artboard on which you want to link your layer.

There is an option to edit Links. Using Animation buttons, you can decide how your link's transition looks like in the Inspector. Using the Target drop-down menu, you can change the Artboards for adding a link. You can also scroll and go back to the previous Artboard by selecting the previous Artboard in the Target drop-down menu. It proves helpful in case you have multiple Artboards linking to a single Artboard.

You can also remove a link. For this, you need to choose **Prototypes > Removes Links from the Selection**. You can achieve this by either setting your link's target to none or by clicking on the trash in the Prototyping section of the Inspector. This will help in removing a link.

ADDING HOTSPOT

It lets you create a clickable area more prominent than a single layer, and it also gives you more control than links. You can choose the **Insert > Hotspot** to insert a hotspot. Alternatively, you can press H and draw your hotspot area by the click and drag method. You can choose the Artboard which you wish to link to the Hotspot. You can go to the Inspector and edit the Hotspot's animation and target Artboard. It is very similar to adding links.

In fact, you can also turn a link into a Hotspot. You can do this by choosing the link and then clicking on the create Hotspot icon, and your job is done. It will turn a link into Hotspot in the Inspector.

You may also fix the position of the Hotspot. First of all, you need to select your Hotspot, and then you need to choose **fix position while scrolling**. It is done in the Inspector. It will fix the position on the Canvas, and the rest of the layers scroll.

The next concept we are going to learn is how to use the Hotspots with Symbol. You can include a Hotspot as a part of the symbol, and you can reuse that symbol. If you don't want to link a hotspot to another Artboard, then there is an option to override the hotspots. You can choose the **View > Prototype > Show all** to show all links and Hotspot. Alternatively, you can also press Ctrl + F. Similarly, you can select **View > Prototype > Hide all** to hide the different paths that represent prototyping links. You can choose **View > Prototype > Show with Selection** to see the Links and Hotspots between what you have selected. Alternatively, you can also press Ctrl + Alt + F. You can use preferences in Canvas to change their color, those have already been discussed in the Canvas.

HOW TO CREATE FIXED ELEMENTS?

You need to select a layer or Hotspot in order to create fixed elements. You can check in the **Fix position when scrolling** option in the prototyping section in the Inspector. There is also an alternate way to do the same, and you can choose the **Prototype > Fixed layer position when scrolling in the menu**. If you want to fix a row of tabs at the bottom of an app design or in case you have a floating button on the website.

You can also go for creating a scrolling Artboard. You can choose an Artboard preset if you want to create a prototype with a scrolling Artboard. You can also create a custom preset and resize its height. Your Prototype won't scroll if you're going to use a preset and draw a custom Artboard instead. You can select the preset and change its height in the Canvas to create a scrolling prototype from an Artboard preset. You can include the word resize in the Inspector.

You can choose to **Create Custom Size** at the bottom of the Inspector to create a custom size Artboard preset that scrolls. You can change the height of the Artboard after mentioning its dimensions in the Inspector. The name in the Inspector changes to include the word resized like the regular presets.

HOW TO MAINTAIN SCROLL POSITION AFTER THE CLICK?

Typically, the scrolling artboard position returns to the top (the start position) when you play the Prototype and click on it. It usually happens when you create a Link from one Scrolling Artboard to another. It is okay if we take the cases such as switching the tabs in the mobile app, but it is not good if we take the point where we want to display a modal or overlay in place of the top of the scrolling content.

You need to select the link and click on the **maintain scroll position after clicking** the option in the Inspector if you want to make sure a scrolling Artboard stays in the position when you click on the Prototype.

It lets the scrolling content remain in the same position when we enable this option. This happens when you click on the links and transition between the Artboards.

This will help in the interruption of the Prototype's flow and feel more realistic.

In the next section, we are going to learn about the use of start points and how to use them. It lets you choose which Artboards your prototypes start with when you preview them. You can open your prototypes in the preview window to set a start point. You can go to the drop-down menu, you can select an Artboard. You will always see the Artboard, which you have set as the start point. You can remove the start point by selecting the Artboard and then click on the flag again.

You can set multiple start points. If your design is more complex and you want to guide people through the different aspects of the design. Let's say you want to make the experience of the user flow and the signup flow. All the newly set start points will have a different appearance as an additional prototype in the same document in the app.

PREVIEWING AND SHARING PROTOTYPES

You can preview prototypes in three different ways. They are through the mac app, web app, and iOS device using a mirror.

For previewing the Prototype in the mac app, you shall click on the **Preview** button in the toolbar. Your prototypes will start from the start point which you have set, or else if you have not given the start point, then it starts automatically from the currently selected Artboard. You have to follow specific steps for previewing prototypes:

1. You can see the preview by tapping the target after clicking anywhere in the preview window. You will be able to see the links and hotspots which are available on the current Artboard.

2. If you wish to go back to the previous Artboard, then you can use the **back button**.

3. Similarly, if you want to jump between the Artboards, then you can choose **Artboards drop-down menu**.

4. You can set the current Artboard by using the **flag icon**.

5. If you want to copy a link and share that with others, then you can choose **The Share icon**.

The next thing we are going to look at is how to preview the Prototype in the web app. You can see the prototypes available at the top of the document overview when you open the document in the web app. It shall be noted that you shall make sure that you define the start point else. This will not work in the Web app.

You can enable comments in the document. Anyone can choose to **View Artboard** at the window to leave the Prototype, and they can switch to a static view of the Artboard. You can also add comments there, and the comments will appear in the sidebar. You can choose to close the Prototype and return it to the document.

Preview a Prototype in Mirror

You can launch the mirror app on the iOS device and connect it to USB or Wi-Fi. From there, you can select the notification bell.

If we talk about the sketch mirror app, then we can say that it is a companion to the Sketch app. It requires the Sketch app in addition to work. It also lets you preview sketch designs on iOS devices. You can connect to the Mac app and then navigate between pages and Artboards. It enables you to design up or down intelligently to fit the screen of the iOS devices.

There is no limitation on the number of devices on which we can run the sketch mirror. Bohemian Coding provides it. It requires iOS 11.0 or a later version. It is available in the English language and has a minimal size of 13MB.

You need the link's permission to view in the documents setting to share a prototype.

If we talk about sharing, you need to tap on the share icon on the top of the window at the right corner. It is easy to copy links to the Prototype and then to the clipboard. There is also the freedom to choose any other option on the menu.

You need to note that it is only possible to share prototypes that are available inside the workspace.

The next thing we are going to look at is how to share a prototype in the web app. You can share the link to the Prototype if you want to share the Prototype with other people. You can copy the Prototype of the link from the browser as you are using the web app. Alternatively, you can also copy it by hovering over the thumbnail in the document overview and then click on the three dots that appear there. There, you will get two options:

1. You can share prototypes with the Hotspot. There is the possibility to highlight the Hotspots or links in the Prototype. This will make the user aware of where to click.

2. You can also share prototypes without hotspots. There won't be any hotspots or links visible during the preview session.

You can preview your Prototype in the mirror by tapping on the Artboard. You can navigate to the Prototype by tapping on the links and hotspots. Alternatively, you can close it by swapping it down on the Artboard.

IMPORTING AND EXPORTING

You will learn how to export SVG and CSS code from any browser. You can discover Export presets and slices. You will learn how to import other files into mac app. You can import a file by directly dragging and dropping them into the Canvas. This is the easiest method of all. You can import the following items:

1. SVG and EPS file.

2. You can import PNG, JPG, TIFF, and bitmap images.

3. You can import SVG code. You need to do copy/paste in it to create a layer.

4. You can import PDF documents.

5. You can also import AI and PSD files.

You can choose **Share > Export** as the quickest way to export the work from the mac app. Alternatively, you can press the ⌘ + ⇧ + E, and this will open the export option. You can click on the Export after selecting the item you want to export. You will see File Successfully exported in the bottom part of the canvas once you are done with exporting the assets. You can directly go to the folder where your assets are by clicking on the arrow in the message – the mac app sends the actual size as default and in the PNG format. You can export it as PDF also by holding them ⌥ while dragging the document to export. You can also do this by selecting a layer and then pressing the ⌘ + E. You can choose the **File > Export Artboard as PDF** to export the Artboard as PDF. You can set the preference to another artboard to export. You can check the development handoff to download the asset and inspect the design.

Creating and Using Export Presets

You can choose the layer and make the document exportable at the bottom of the Inspector. This is done in order to export a layer within your document in different sizes or formats. You can choose the presets from the available default presets which appear there. These are the following:

1. **Size:** You can type directly in the size field to create your own, or you can also get the length from the drop-down menu. You can scale up to 1x, 2x and scale down it to 0.25x, 0.5x, and infinitely. You can also define a specific height and width in pixel.

2. **Prefix/Suffix:** You need to provide prefix/suffix at the time of exporting. You can also customize this by typing before or after the eclipse, which represents the file name.

3. **Format:** You can choose a format from the drop-down menu.

4. **Remove presets:** You can click on the X to remove the presets.

5. **Adding presets:** You can use + to add another layer to the export documents.

6. **Set presets:** You can choose the predefined presets. You can also create new presets and remove them too.

7. **Create a Slice:** You can create a slice directly to the layer by clicking on the slice icon.

8. **Export Selected:** You can choose this particular to export.

9. **Preview:** It let you see the preview before your layer looks like.

10. **Sharing:** You can share via mail, messages, and airdrop, etc.

Using Slices

You can export anything within the Slices, and they are created by drawing on the Canvas. You can perform various different functions such as select, resize, move, and hide, just like the different layers. You can insert a slice by choosing the **Insert > Slice**, or alternatively, you can also press S to do the same. You can draw a new slice by dragging anywhere on the Canvas. You shall give the descriptive name in the layer list in the mac app. This shall be provided at the time of creating a slice. You can use/in the name, the mac app anything you write before/ as the folder name, and anything after that/will be the file name. You can also set multiple export presets for the slices. You will find the option when you select a slice in the Inspector. If you want to remove the empty pixel around the edges of the slice's content, then click on **Trim transparent pixel**. You can place a slice on within-group and check export group content only. It will include the content from within the slice group for slice group export. You can apply background color to the slice exports.

You can export CSS and SVG code. You can select any layer in the document, do the control-click, and then choose the **Copy CSS Attribute**. It can copy the style format the document has as the CSS code. I am giving a sample CSS code.

Background: #6dd400;

Border-radius: 5px;

You can copy the SVG code in the same way by selecting a shape layer and then choosing to **Copy SVG Code**.
Mac app support to the following file format:

1. **Bitmap:** They are a flattened version of any export in the mac app. They open as a single layer in other apps. A sketch can export to the following bitmap format: PNG, JPG, TIFF, and WebP. You may see more options depending on the file format you choose. You can use the Save for web to strip out the additional field data. It is data from the image such as EXIF metadata. By interlacing the PNG, it is possible to load the full size as soon as possible, and for the total quality, they can download more data. Progressive JPGs are not clear but blurry at the start, but later on, they become sharp. The lower quality image is smaller in size for JPG and WebP.

2. **Vector:** They preserve layers and paths. It is straightforward to edit them and work with them. The app supports the SVG, PDF, and EPS formats. You can choose Copying SVG code. You can use the

control-click method to copy/paste the SVG code. Some features are not supported in the format, such as transparent gradient in PDFs.

SHORTCUTS

It increases the speed of the workflow. Here is the list of shortcuts:

General Shortcuts

a. ⌘ C: It is used for copying.

b. ⌘ X: It is used to cut the data.

c. ⌘ V: It is used to paste the data.

d. ⌘ ⇧ V: It is used to paste over the selection.

e. Space drag: It is used in pan canvas.

f. ⌘ ⇧ N: It is used for a new page.

g. fn ↑:   It lets you go to previous page.

h. fn ↓:   It lets you go to next page.

i. ⌘ +:   It is used to zoom in.

j. ⌘ -   It is used to zoom out.

k. Ctrl R   It will show/hide rulers.

l. Ctrl P   It is used to show/hide pixels.

m. Ctrl X   It is used to show/hide pixel grid.

n. Ctrl G   It is used to show/hide the grid.

o. Ctrl L   It is used to show/hide the layout grid.

p. Ctrl E	It is used to show/hide slices.
q. Ctrl F	It is used to show all hotspot and links.
r. Ctrl ⌥ F	It will show hotspot link for selected artboard, layers, or group.
s. Ctrl 1 2	It lets you switch between canvas and component view.
t. ⌘ F	It lets you filter in layer list and components view.
u. ⌘123	It lets you switch between components types in comp.
v. ⌘ Ctrl K	You can run the custom plugin.
w. ⌘ Z	You can undo.
x. ⌘ ⇧ Z	It lets you redo.
y. ⌘ N	It lets you open new documents.
z. ⌘ O,	It lets you open the documents window.
aa. ⌘ ⇧ O,	It lets you open the local document window.
bb. ⌘ W	It lets you close the window.
cc. ⌘ S	It lets you save the document.
dd. ⌘ ⇧ S	It lets you duplicate the document.
ee. ⌘ ⌥ ⇧ S	It lets you perform save as function.
ff. ⌘ ⇧ P	It lets you do page setup.
gg. ⌘,	It lets you open preferences.

hh. ⌘ H	It lets you hide the mac app.
ii. ⌘ Q	It lets you quit the mac app.
jj. ⌘ ⇧?	It lets you open the help menu.
kk. ⌘ P	It lets you an open prototyping preview window.
ll. ⌘⇧,	It lets you open the document setting window.

Insert Layers

mm. R	It is used for inserting rectangle.
nn. O	It is used for inserting oval.
oo. L	It is used for inserting a line.
pp. You	It is used for the rounded rectangle.
qq. V	It is a vector tool.
rr. P	It lets you insert a pencil tool.
ss. T	It is used for text tool.
tt. A	It is used for artboard tool.
uu. S	It is used for slice tool.
vv. H	It is used for hotspot tool.
ww. C	It is used to open insert window.
xx. Enter	It lets you insert selected components from canvas.
yy. Enter	You can go to selected symbol's source.

zz. ⌥ drag	It lets you draw a new shape from the center.
aaa. ⇧ drag	It lets you lock the ratio of shapes.
bbb. Space drag	It lets you move a new layer before you place it.

COLOR PROFILES

It basically describes how the colors shall be rendered in an image. You can maintain accuracy across different screens using a color profile. The color appears as a number of a different scale to designers, such as white is 255,255,255, and it gives the maximum amount of the lights adding up to white. You shall take into account that every display is different, so it complicates the process. The display can show darker and light colors as the technology improves. It will let you maintain consistency across the various displays. You can think of them as matching numbers with the real-world colors. They make sure that the color appears the same across every screen as much as possible.

They are attached to the images and are used by the applications to interpret the numbers in pictures into visible colors. The accurate preview depends on what color space you are viewing in the document. Color space-attached image to ensure the destination application (for example, a web browser) has the correct information to interpret it. You can work in different color profiles depending on the project. You can check which color profile matches your needs.

Unmanaged Color Profile

Mac uses the unmanaged color profile to make things simple. It is by default in mac app. Your system default color profile is used, such as color LCD on a MacBook pro. You shall not call for a profile if you don't want to manage your color profile. You can use the default preference as they are.

Older machines app have better performance benefits, but there is a drawback that when you export files; the color may look different than what you see on the mac app. Those images exported in unmanaged documents get tagged with the sRGB color profile to ensure consistent display across various applications and devices. You can choose between sRGB and P3 color profiles if you need to work in a specific color profile.

sRGB Color Profile

sRGB is most likely the option to choose if you are designing for a web or for a wide variety of output displays. W3C standard and sRGB are used by every modern web browser. Almost all phones, Macs, and most screens are capable of displaying the colors. It will give you consistent color across screens.

Display P3 Profile

sRGB was the only color space used for quite a long time by designers. This practice has changed with the introduction of a wide gamut of displays that can render more vibrant colors. Now there is a display of a much larger number of expressible colors. All this has led to the introduction of a new color profile called a display P3 profile. If you would like to use more vibrant colors available and target the devices that support display P3 color profile and if your projects include heavy video or photos, then it would be best to use this color profile. You will not be able to see the more vibrant and brighter color in display P3 if you are not using a wide gamut of display yourself at the time of creating designs. It makes working in the Display P3 color profile difficult, so there is a suggestion to stick to the sRGB or unmanaged profile in such a case. When you export an image out of the P3 profile, the exported image will also have an attached P3 profile. You shall consider the final medium on which your sketch works. It is not inherently better than sRGB due to its new and wide gamut of colors. You can choose your profile on the output medium above all. It will not be a good idea to provide P3 images if you know they can only be displayed on a screen that can display nothing wider than an sRGB profile. It becomes essential if you are working on P3 capable machines because it will disappoint you when you see images used in the final product.

You have to be very careful about when to choose a color profile or when to go unmanaged. It depends on the project you are working on, and accordingly, you select a specific color profile or go with the unmanaged mac default profile. Make sure that the file you are exporting does not have the same color profile as the default one. Picking a color profile can be a good idea if you are working with a team using multiple macs and display profiles. It helps in maintaining consistency across all those screens. Editing documents in mac app can be slower on some lower-end mac without a discrete GPU. It happens when you assign a color profile instead of unmanaged mode.

You have to consider a lot of points while choosing a color profile and in deciding whether to use a color profile or not. You can change the default profile from the unmanaged in the **preference > canvas > color profile**. You will get a notification if the color profile is different than the default. You can change the color profile of an existing document in a sketch very quickly. You can choose **File > Document Setting**. You can pick the color profile you want to use and select the canvas. You will end up with two options. You can assign a new color to the document, or you can convert every color to a new color space. The option you choose will determine how you want the colors in the final image. You can think about when you should assign a color profile and when you should convert. You will keep the same RGB values from one profile to another when you set new color to your document. Visual appearance in the document changes slightly, especially the bright colors, but the RGB values remains intact. Suppose if you are working in an unmanaged or sRGB profile and if you wish to change your profile to display P3, the images will appear alongside the other Display P3 content and then you want to assign new color space to preserve the RGB values. It is a non-destructive process to change color from the sRGB to the Display P3 color profile. You can convert back and forth as you are not changing the underlying RGB values.

DEVELOPER HANDOFF

It is the next step of the design process. Sketch does use third-party tools to make developer handoffs. In this section, we are going to look at the organizing designs, staying in sync, and sharing them with the people inside and outside the workspace. You can hand off powerful designs to developers and you can provide them with the necessary things, and this will make your design a product. After you are done with the prototyping, sharing, and testing of the design, you can hand over the work to the developer and they will give life to your design. This step has a certain limitation and that is the lack of proper information given to the developer. This might result in a mismatch between what you made and the final implementation. It may turn a product into the worst product and might hinder the speed of the product. They can get sometimes slow. The handoff tools in sketch come free of cost and you can collaborate with the developer at no extra cost. The developer doesn't require any mac app or the third plugins for the work part.

You can find specific details of the design in a web Inspector. It helps the developer to examine all the details about each element in the design. You can find all the relevant attributes in the Inspector by clicking on the artboard or layer in the web app. You can get each detail from the positioning to the color variables. It is also achievable for the developers to measure the spacing between layers from the artboard itself. They can also inspect groups or several layers that are within them. It is easy to point out to each part of the design as a web inspector level every single element in your design. Developers use comments and threads right in the web app to communicate their queries. They make things as clear as possible. Handoff has become more effortless with workspaces. The spacing between the elements and clear information is available. The developers can inspect your designs by using any browser or operating system. They do not require mac app for operating.

They will be able to inspect any design if you add them as viewers and they do not need third-party plugins for this. You can invite them if you are working outside your workspace. It does not cost you any extra charges as they are included. The developer can copy attributes and color variables in just one click. Developers need the information during their handoff. It is the reason that the web app inspector provides a copy of any attributes value and it gets clipped to your clipboard. These include color and text attributes. You can choose any attribute by hovering over it and clicking on it. Developers have a different format to choose from when copying colors and color variables. They choose according to what suits them best. You can check the library or color variable's group and it helps you to refer at any time you need.

You can download product-ready assets at your convenience. The developers get the images and icons they need through Inspector. There is an option to mark assets as exportable in the mac app. They can be downloaded very easily. Developers have access to the most up-to-date and updated version of assets. They have also expertise on where to find what. There are options available to the developers to choose whether individual assets or whole assets. They have the freedom to choose the file format. You can enable the web app Inspector for anyone you share them with from the documents menu.

We have already learned how to Inspect layers. You can find the current artboard's attribute in the right side Inspector including background colors and layout settings. You can see the properties of any layers by just selecting them and seeing their properties in the Inspector. You can control-click over the layer which you want to select and choose it from the contextual menu if there is any case of layer overlap. Inspector automatically updates to display the attribute if you select any layer. It all depends on the type of layers and value of an attribute that you select and that will appear in the sidebar. You can see the basic parameter if you inspect, let's say borders. You can find the color, position, as well as other border options such as dashes, gaps, or join styles. Some things are hidden to make things simple such as 100% opacity or normal blend mode. MacOS coordinate system is used in the mac app. It is equivalent to 1 pixel as one point. The point in the mac app is similar to the CSS px measurements.

You can Inspect Symbols as a developer. The symbol which is selected on the artboard is highlighted and a card for it is shown in the Inspector. You can also choose the symbol name from the contextual menu by just selecting the symbol and control-clicking on the layer. You can jump to its source if the symbol that you chose is a part of the library in the workspace. You can do this by just clicking the symbol's name and arrow icon on the artboard or in the Inspector. You can get the latest version of the symbol even if you are using the older version of the document. You will get the highlight if you select a layer within the nested symbol or nested symbol itself. You can also get the information related to the nested symbol in the Inspector bar. You can use the symbol card in the sidebar to head to the symbol source or you can go to the arrow in the artboard. You cannot inspect a symbol source if that is part of the library that is not saved in the workspace. But you can see the symbol name and the path of the library. You can press the back button in the browser to go back to the artboard if you are finished viewing or inspecting a symbol source.

The developer can measure the distance between layers. You can choose the artboard and then hover over to the display measurements that show relative distance between them. You can copy the layer attribute by hovering over to the layer and clicking on the attribute. You can see the notification to confirm it. The value is copied if you are copying the single attribute. The attribute with multiple values such as color opacity, angle, and gradient types will give value and attribute names to the clipboard. You will get the name and path copied to the clipboard when you copy a text style or a layer style. You can see the details of the selected text styles or layer styles in the sidebar. You can get the full path of the shared style we have selected. You can hover over to the layer style or text style can copy them. You can also copy multiple attribute values. For example, all the values of shadow or values that build text layer. You can hover over the heading above the group and then click on the values. This way you can copy all the values of the layers selected. You can copy the text to the clipboard by going to the content section in the Inspector. You can hover over the documents and click on them. Anyone who can inspect or edit the document can also download the document assets and set them as exportable. You can request for assets export. There is a provision to export individual assets. You can go to the artboard in the web app and then choose to inspector tab on the right. You can bring up the Inspector attribute by clicking on the layer on the artboard. You can find the export options at the bottom of the sidebar provided the layer has the export options set in the original sketch. You can download the layer in that format by clicking on the download button next to export options. You can choose to download all the assets in all formats, sizes, and resolutions.

If the export section is not shown in the Inspector, then it might be possible that the exportable layer is hidden behind another layer or within any group. You can export all the assets.

COMMENT AND NOTIFICATION

Comments and threads are used to get feedback from the colleague, stakeholder, or anyone with whom you share your design. Using these comments and ideas come together in one place.

Commenting on Documents

Comments can be added to any documents across the artboard in a workspace document. It can be done in the web app. You can view the artboard in the sidebar, which is on the right side. You can show/hide it by clicking on the sidebar icon on the top right corner. You can select to see the activity in the sidebar. You can add comments and check comments there. You can edit or delete a comment by hovering over the three dots and choosing the requisite action. There is option to use emojis in your comments and even replies with them. Comments are enabled for all documents by default. You can disable them, or for a specific document, you need to go to the cog icon in the top-right, and then you need to choose document setting from there. You can perform the uncheck comments operations there and then save the final document.

Comments Thread

If you want to reply to a comment which is outside of the main feed, then you can use threads; they make help in organizing the discussion and also keep an eye on the different conversations. You can reply to the comment by clicking on the thread and clicking on the link underneath it. You can post a comment by typing it and then pressing the ⌘ Enter. You can see the number of replies to the comments that have already threads, and you will not know the reply link. You can choose the X Comments to link to open up the thread.

Manage Comments Notification

There is an option to choose notification for few comments on a specific thread, single artboard, or the whole documents. There is by default notification for every document on which you comment, but this can be changed at any time. Suppose you want to receive notification for the whole documents. In that case, you choose to go to the document's overview page and then select follow this document in the drop-down menu in the sidebar. You can stop receiving the notification by choosing to stop following these documents. You can open a specific artboard, and if you want to follow notifications for it, then you can choose to follow this artboard from the drop-down menu in the menu bar.

View Comment Notifications

You can go to the update tab in the left sidebar to access all the notifications. You can find all the replies and mention them on the update page to which you have subscribed.

You can read in context or reply. You can also jump to a specific artboard and read the comments related there. You can choose to mark a notification as read or choose to mark all as read.

CONCLUSION

In this chapter, we saw Prototyping in Sketch. We learned how to add Links and add Hotspot. Then, we learned to create Fixed Elements. We learned to maintain scroll position after the click. We also learned about Previewing and Sharing Prototype. We learned about the Importing and Exporting Sketch file.

CHAPTER 7

Real-Time Collaboration

IN THIS CHAPTER

➢ Understanding the fundamentals of Real-Time Collaboration

➢ Understanding the requirements of Real-Time Collaboration

➢ Learning how to save the document

➢ Understanding how to invite people to Collaborate

➢ Getting familiar with working and editing in the real-time

In the previous chapter, we learned about Prototyping. We learned about adding links and hotspots. We understood how to create fixed elements and how to maintain a scroll

DOI: 10.1201/9781003261575-7

position after the click. We saw sharing and previewing prototypes. We learned about previewing a prototype in a mirror.

In this chapter, we will learn the Real-Time Collaboration. We will see how to save the document. We will retain the technique of inviting people to collaborate. We will see working and Editing in real time.

The real benefit of working in real time is seeing the other's work and learning from there. There is no worry about editing the correct version of the document.

REQUIREMENTS FOR REAL-TIME COLLABORATION

You will require the following things to edit documents in real time:

1. First of all, you need a **Subscription**. It is included as a part of the subscription. This is not similar to the macOS license, so you need to verify whether you have a subscription or not. You can go to choose the **Sketch > Preference** and then go to the **Account** tab. You will see that you are a member of the list below your profile picture if you already subscribed. You can find more information from the **Setting** options.

2. You can have the document in a shared workplace. You can move the current documents from My Drafts to a shared workplace. This will make the document shareable. Alternatively, you can use the mac app. It would be best to go to the **Windows > Documents** or press ⇧ + ⌘ + O. The next step is to drag and drop the

document to the relevant project in the sidebar. You shall always make a backup for the documents.

3. You need a compatible version of mac app. In such a case, I suggest you use mac version 71 or later as they are compatible. It would be best if you learned that only a compatible version of the mac app would be able to open the document.

You can use mac app 71 or a later version to get started with the real-time Collaboration in the document. You shall save the documents so that it is available in the workspace.

SAVING THE DOCUMENTS

As I told you, you need to save the document in the workspace in order to use the collaborate feature. You can choose the **File > Save**, or alternatively, you can also press ⌘ + S. Then, you need to select the tab which appears as

to a workspace and then save it and choose the workspace where you want to store it.

You can choose the **Collaboration** item in the toolbar, and then you can choose to save it to a workspace. There is a popover menu from which you can choose.

You can make an existing document more compatible by saving it in the workspace. You need to move your document and save it in a shared workspace. You will need to open it in the mac version 71 or later to run it successfully. However, there will be an automatic prompt from the mac app to do this. The people using the mac version 71 or older will be able to see it once you are done with saving the document appropriately. After that, you will open it in the older version, but you can save it only locally. In order to make it editable where everyone can edit, you need to embed any fonts while sharing the File.

INVITING PEOPLE TO COLLABORATE

If the File is saved in the shared workspace, then everyone who is there in that workspace can see it. The editor can start opening it in the mac app and collaborate with it. There is also an opportunity to invite the outside people and let them collaborate in the workspace by giving them access. In order to collaborate, they must fulfill the criteria of having a mac app version 71.

You can manage share settings. You can go to the document setting, click on the Collaborate item, and choose the Share Document option. It is elementary to control the setting. Using the web app, you need to click on the three dots in the thumbnail of the document and then select the **Document Setting**. You can set it as a library under the general tab. People outside the workspace can come to View, edit your document as a guest. This is done under the sharing tab. You can also provide a public link to make the record shareable.

It does alter the subscription if you are inviting people from outside the workspace.

You can share the document via mail. You can enter the person's mail id with whom you want to share the document, and you can select the type of access you want to give to such person from the drop-down menu. There is an autocomplete option for the person who is already in the workspace. You can quickly select their name. But if you want to include some outside person, you need to type his email, and select add option sent an invitation email.

You can choose different access levels when you share the document with anyone. Following are the options.

1. **View:** It lets you view the document and leave comments.

2. **Inspect:** It enables you to inspect the web app's layers and Artboards for handoffs and assets.

3. **Edit:** It lets you the option to open and edit to the collaborator.

It generally appears in the shared with me section to the person with whom you shared the documents. You can find an invite pending badge next to the person you sent the invitation as a guest. This will appear until they accept the invitation. For permanent members, they have to be an admin to get the badge. There is also a secure option to withdraw access given to someone or remove their access. It is one of the cool features. You can provide a public link as access. You have different options such as no access, view the document, inspect the document, and enable comments on the Artboards.

If you are using the web version, then you can click on the cog icon in the top right corner of the screen. You can choose the Document settings and then select the Sharing and Permissions. Here, you can give link settings in various forms, such as they can view, edit, inspect, or comment.

If you are using the mac app, then click on the three dots and then choose the **Share Document**. The document opens in the web app and you can see the window described above.

You need to open the document in order to collaborate. In the mac app, you can choose the **File > Open Workspace Document**. You can open the document from the document window. If you are using the web app, then you need to choose the link you received to access it. You can then select the **Edit** in the bottom right corner. You can find the last person's name who worked on the document from the document window. You can find the person who is currently working with the documents, and their names appear next to the word Editing. You can find its live status by opening the activity feed.

WORKING AND EDITING IN REAL TIME

There will be a collaboration menu and cursors if you are working in real time. There are three avatars of active collaborators in the toolbar. There appear the colors of their cursor on the canvas. You can open the menu by clicking on the three dots in the toolbar above the Collaboration. You can find the list of all editors working on the documents as well as you will get some of the valuable sharing options. You will find a colored ring around someone who is active. It will appear around their avatars. You can click on the avatars' names in the toolbar to hide or show the cursors or names of the collaborators. You can choose the **Show Collaborators Cursors/Names** to hide/show your collaborators.

You can open the activity feed and find if someone is currently working on the document in the shared workspace. In case the Collaboration does not appear in the toolbar, then you can make it appear in the toolbar by choosing the **View > Customize toolbar**, and then you can use the drag and drop option from there.

We will be discussing the Editing in real time. As you know, when you collaborate in real time, then you can see who is working on it or not. You can see other's edits once they are done with the Editing. There is no option to see the edit happening pixel by pixel, but you can see it once it is completed. There is also a superb option where one or more collaborators can edit the same layer simultaneously. But you shall not make redo/undo, or it will create a mess there. There is also an option to override the other's changes if they perform the Edit immediately after you Edit. But you shall avoid editing the same layer at the same time if in case you see another's the cursor.

Follow Mode

You can open the collaborator menu and click on the other's avatars if you want to follow someone else as they collaborate with you in the document. In such a case, your canvas will match with the View of the person whom you are following. There is also an option to display their names at the top and outlines them. The person gets the notification in the mac app that you are following him/her.

There might be several reasons in case you are unable to follow someone:

1. The person might be inactive.

2. They might leave a document.

3. They may have made any such private settings.

4. They are following someone else or you.

If someone whom you followed becomes inactive, then you are no longer following him. You cannot see their cursor if they leave the document. You can only see their canvas view. You can zoom in or click anywhere on the canvas to stop following someone. You can also set your preferences. You can choose whether or not you want people to follow you or keep your setting private instead of public. You can click on your avatar and then select the **Allow users to follow you**. Alternatively, you can choose the **View > Canvas > Allow users to follow you**.

You can save documents during Collaboration. The documents are basically synced so everyone who is collaborated in the document can see each other in real time. If anyone opens the documents, then he will get the latest updates automatically. You can take snapshots of the document as a new update every time, or else the document is sync automatically. It is possible to see what others created as an update. They appear in the web app as document timelines. You can mark an update as necessary by celebrating it as a star. You can, at the same time, make it visible to viewers.

Although editing the document in the workspace is recommended, you can download the document and edit it locally. You can then upload the edited document. You can work offline in the workspace, but once you are back online, then all the changes made to the documents will automatically sync. What to do when we close the mac app? Do we need to save it? The answer is no. The mac app automatically collects the latest updates and places them into new updates in a file, and the documents are saved in the workspace automatically.

Alternatively, you can save the latest updates manually too. You can do this by pressing the ⌘ + S or choosing the **File > Save**. This will help in creating new updates of the document in the workspace. The users who use the shared document can comment on and inspect the versions for handoff.

MANAGING DOCUMENTS

In this section, we are going to learn about managing the different operations with the documents. We will see from saving to using versioning in the workspace. You can open workspace documents in the mac app. You can do it by the document window in the mac app to open and find the documents. You can open any documents in mac app by just double-clicking on it. You will get to see the document window every time you will open the mac app. You can also open a workspace document in the document window. You can do this by choosing the **File > Open Workspace documents**, or alternatively, you can press the ⌘ + O key. You can find these things in the sidebar if you are part of a team or create projects. You can find the document by clicking on the workspace or project name. It will show all the documents that belong to it. You can find the project document under the thumbnail of the document window. You can find different levels of access that the document has with the following icons:

1. It can be accessed by anyone who has the document's link.

2. It allows a particular guest to access it.

3. The third one is only me. That means only you can access the documents.

You can use a switcher in the top left of the window to toggle between the workspaces. You can use the new templates or create any new project. It can be done from the component window.

You can use the web app to open and edit documents. You can go to the documents overview at the bottom of the sidebar to open any document directly from the browser, and for that, you need to click on the Edit button. It might need to confirm the action before you can open the document in the mac app. It generally depends on the browser. You can find a new icon to the right of the zoom control to open the documents if you are using the single Artboard. You need to be focused on that specific Artboard. You can also use all documents view in the workspace to open a document from the mac app. You can edit the document by hovering over the document's thumbnail.

Create a New Document

You can double-click on the new document thumbnail to create it in the document window. You can choose **File > New**. Alternatively, you can press ⌘ + N for creating a new document.

The next thing is saving the document. For this, you need to choose the **File > Save** or press the ⌘ + S button in order to save the document. Then you need to select a workspace by selecting a workspace tab. Here, you want to save the document. You will find the project folder too.

While saving the document if you close, you will be asked whether you want to save the document or close and cancel the save. The update will not upload to the workspace if you choose to complete and cancel the save. You can also use the Collaborate button in the toolbar to save a document to the workspace. You can select a workspace and a project to save. You need to click on the Save button.

You can save the document, which is saved locally to your location to the workspace, by dragging and dropping the documents into the document window to save it to the workspace. You can then choose a workspace and save the document in that workspace. If you are moving your entire documents to your workspace, then it's no issue as it works with multiple documents. You can save the files locally by choosing the **File > Save**. Alternatively, you can also press the ⌘ + S. You need to go to the mac tab and choose the location where you want the File to be saved. You can also save the documents in real time. You need to save it to the workspace if you're going to collaborate the documents. The work is saved automatically while we are working once we save the work to the workspace. There will be an update when you close or save a document. There will be some things like snapshots of the work at the moment. You can use the web app's sidebar to access and browse the update. You can download the document while you are working with others. You can make changes to their documents or any updates locally and manually, and then you can upload them to the workspace as new versions of the documents. You can click on the update before uploading the document. It might overwrite edits from the other collaborators, and you are asked about it every time before uploading the documents. Let's say that someone is working on the same document as yours; if they are done, only then you can push the changes in the documents. You can save the real-time collaboration document offline too. Your changes are saved locally when you are working offline. But once you are online again, the modifications stored offline will come as online and automatically sync in the workspace. The latest version of the documents will contain all the changes. If you are offline and someone deletes the objects you have edited, then there won't be any changes that users can apply to that object.

How to Use Updates

You can make changes to the document in the workspace and store that document locally. When you open the web app, the changes appear automatically as the new update in the sidebar. You can view the older version by clicking on the update in the sidebar. You can go to the top right side and click on the see the latest version, so if you were using an older version, then you can check or see the newest version from there itself. You can use the Artboard View to see the specific updates for the particular Artboard.

You can also delete the update in the sidebar by hovering over the update. The next thing you need to do is to click on the three dots and then select the **Delete** option. This will help in the deletion of any update. There appears the confirmation window which will ask you to confirm the updates delete, and then it finally deletes the updates. There is also a note to be taken that you cannot delete if there is only one update in the document's history.

How to Switch between Workspaces?

It would be best if you were a workspace member or guest to switch between those workspaces. You need to go to the drop-down menu in the top left sidebar of the document window if you are using mac app. You can choose toggle between workspace using the ⌘1 button. You can use the number corresponding to your workspace. In that workspace, you can see the documents and projects related to that workspace. You can select your workspace in the web app from the drop-down menu on the left side. You can view all the documents there themselves. You can view workspace documents in the web app. You can use the Collaborate option in the toolbar and choose **File > Workspace,** and then you can select the **View in Workspace**. You can open the document in the new document window. You can choose the workspace of the drop-down menu in the top left of the web app if someone has shared a document with you via workspace email address. You can go to the right panel and find the documents there. If anyone has shared a link with you for their workspace, then you need to click on that link, and it will open it up in the browser. You can find the Artboards, prototypes, pages, and Symbols once you open the document in the web app. You can view them in more detail by going over them. You can view a particular page Artboard by going to the drop-down menu in the document's title. You can browse the document in either list or a grid view. There is a button in the top right corner of the web app menu to switch between these two views. You can jump between the different Artboards by clicking on the arrows on the top left side or using arrow keys to view an individual Artboard. You can view the full size of an individual Artboard by zooming in the individual Artboard. You can also use the zoom control in the top right. You can press the following keys:

0: It will let you zoom to 100%.

1: It will help in fitting the Artboard on the screen.

+: It will let you zoom in.

-: It will let you zoom out.

You can see all the contents by scrolling around.

You can make a local copy of the workspace document. It depends on the AutoSave preference in the mac app whether you want to choose **File > Duplicate** if the Autosave is on. You can also select the **File > Save as** if the Autosave is disabled. It will help in saving a new copy of the document. There is an option to save the document locally or to save it to the workspace. Saving in the workspace lets you collaborate. You will Duplicate in the File menu if your Autosave is enabled, and you can hold the ⌥ to enable the Save As instead. You can hover over to the project and click on the **Download Document** to download the document in the web app from the workspace. You can click on the setting icon in the top right of the document or Artboard view and then choose Download Document.

How to Move Documents from My Draft to Shared Workspace

You can hover over to the document thumbnail in the web app to move the documents from the My Drafts to a shared workspace. You shall select the more option three dots appearing and then choose **a move to project**. You can confirm your move by selecting the project you want your document to move to. It is to be noted that you cannot undo the document moved from My Draft to workspace. Once it is moved, then it is.

You can also add a preview thumbnail to the workspace document. You need to move the Artboard and make it the first Artboard on the first page. It will not appear if it is not 250 × 250 in the dimension at least.

You can download the document from the web app. For doing this, you need to click on the Download Document at the bottom of the sidebar. You can hover over to the document thumbnail, click on the three dots, and choose to download the document.

You can download the latest update by clicking on the Download Document. It works fine, even if that is the older update.

You can rename the document. You can choose the **File > Rename** in the mac app. You can press the enter button after entering the new name in the title bar. You can also rename a document by double-clicking on the document thumbnail in the document window. You can also do this by control-clicking on the thumbnail. You can hover over to the document thumbnail in the web app, click on the three dots, and rename there. This is for the workspace. If you are working on Artboard view, you need to choose the Setting icon in the top right and rename it.

Finally, we are going to see how to delete a document. You can control-click on the document thumbnail in the document window in the mac app and choose from there the option to Delete. You can also press the backspace key on the keyboard after clicking on the thumbnail once.

You can hover over to the workspace or project view thumbnail and click on the three dots if you are working in the web app. You need to choose the **Delete Document** option, and this will delete the document. Alternatively, you can drag and drop the thumbnails item in the trash, and it will do the same. The trash is located in the sidebar.

You can click on the setting if you are viewing the single Artboard. It appears in the top right. You need to choose the **Delete Document** option and done. The documents deleted in the workspace go to trash, and you can permanently delete them from there, or it will automatically delete them permanently from there in 90 days. You can also restore them. You can go to trash and click on the document preview and select the restore option from there. It will relocate to its original place. You can also hover over to the document preview in the trash and choose from that. After clicking on the three dots, you can select the **Restore** option. As I told you, you can permanently delete it from the trash by clicking on the three dots and choosing **Delete Permanently**. It will remove all the activities permanently, and no one can access them anymore. You can also empty the trash by clicking on the three dots and choosing **the empty trash** option. This is the permanent blank. It is only possible to empty trash from the web browser till now, and in the future, it will expand its feature.

CONCLUSION

In this chapter, we learned about the Real-Time Collaboration. We saw requirements for Real-Time Collaboration. We learned saving the documents. We learned inviting people to Collaborate. We understood working and editing in Real Time. We learned managing the documents.

CHAPTER 8

Sketch Extensions

IN THIS CHAPTER

- ➢ Getting Familiar with the Sketch Extensions
- ➢ Understand the Fundamentals of Plugins
- ➢ Understand the Fundamentals of Assistants
- ➢ Learning Integration

In the previous chapter, we learnt about Real-Time Collaborations. We saw the requirements for Real-Time Collaborations. We knew the methods of saving the documents. We learned how to invite people to Collaborate. We learned about working and editing in real time.

In this chapter, we are going to see Sketch Extensions. We will learn the Fundamentals of Plugins. We will learn about the Assistants. Finally, we will know the Integration.

DOI: 10.1201/9781003261575-8

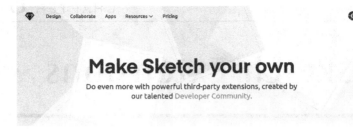

Sketch has more third-party powerful extensions created by its expert developers. It has plugins, Assistants,
and Integrations. You can find out that many assistants
are helping in the design, spotting the issues, and staying
consistent. These assistants are Sketch2React Conventions,
accessibility, organizer, etc. There are hundreds of plugins
that provide extra functionality and automate work. Few
of them are stark, chart, Overflow, plant, Vectary and
Crowdin. Some integrations let you integrate with the
third-party app. Some of them are Lokalise, Maze, Flinto,
Abstract, Overlay, and Zeplin. We will discuss them one
by one.

PLUGINS

They let you expand the app functionality and lets you
do extra works. There are many official sketch plugins,
but most are developed by third-party developers. Some
plugins do not cost anything, and they are free, while at
the same time, you need to purchase some of the plugins
from the developers. You can go to the Extension page and
download a plugin and add it to your sketch work. You
have to double-click on it and install it. You can go to the
plugins menu to access the features of the plugins.

How to Manage and Uninstall Plugins?

You can choose the **Plugins > Manage Plugins**. You can view it in mac app preferences, and from there, you can view plugins documentation, disable it, or remove it altogether.

You can disable plugins with safe mode. There are times when plugins misbehave and cause the app to hang or slow it down. In such a case, you will need to remove the plugins. Otherwise, your mac app may sometimes crash too. You can restart and press the ⇧ button for the inspection of any such cases. You can re-enable all your plugins by continuing the mac app. You can also create a plugin. It let you write the Sketch Plugin in JavaScript. You can access the mac OS framework by taking the help of the ES6.

Plugins also find the use of APIS such as Public JavaScript API and internal API. Plugins are located as folders. A sketch can scan the location of these plugins:

~/Library/Application Support/com.bohemian coding. sketch3/Plugins

After updating the plugins and keeping them in a separate folder:

~Library/Application Support/com.bohemian coding. sketch3/PluginsWarehouse

The Sketch will copy the file in the plugin for you if you double click on it .SketchPlugin file. All the commands following that will show up in the Plugins menu.

You can also install plugins by moving them into the plugins folder.

You can also uninstall plugins by choosing the **Plugins > Manage Plugins** option from the menu.

Plugins are further categorized into three categories. They are Featured Plugins, Official Plugins, and All Plugins.

Featured Plugins

- **Stark:** It lets you design and build products that are accessible, reliable, and inclusive. It provides access to everyone. It enables you to update your existing plans. It is used extensively by designers, Engineers. It lets you inspect the contrast level in your design with a Contrast Checker. It has intelligent color suggestions with AA and AAA passing. It enables you to use vision Simulations. It lets you deep dive into the project's colors using Vision Generator. It allows you to evaluate changes on the fly using Chrome extensions. It simplifies handoffs with sequences.

- **Chart:** It lets you create charts with JSON data or random or tabular data. It enables you to customize the regular View of Charts. You can create graphs, and it saves time. It allows you to visualize data from any source such as tabular data, JSON data, and Random data. Tabular data uses excel, Google Sheets. It lets you copy/paste and link data. JSON data enables you to connect API via HTTPS link. You can create a random data Chart if you don't have the actual data. It supports copy-paste from Google Sheets and excels. You can customize the Charts by applying a color palette, change the thickness and bar width. It lets you use the local or global settings to apply a style. There are different types of charts:

- Line graph.

- Pie Charts.

- Horizontal bars.

- Vertical bars.

- Donut Chart.

- Candlestick chart.

- Group chat.

- Area chart.

- Stream graph.

- The horizontal group bar chart.

- Progress bar.

- Scatter plot.

- Heatmap.

- Histogram.

- Overflow lets you sync and converts the artboards in Overflow, and it changes your design into a playable user flow diagram. It enables you to navigate through easily.

Official Plugins

- **Color Variables Migrator:** It lets you migrate your layer style and use new color variable features from sketch 69. It was introduced in sketch 69, where you can reuse the colors across the documents. It lets you maintain consistency. Sketch automatically convert the papers into a color variable with pre 69 color swatches. It is all dependent on the user whether he wants to migrate layer style or not. The plugins let you update the existing Color Variable. It enables you to edit all text and layer styles to an existing color variable. There is a limitation to plugins working, and that is it works only in current open documents, so if you want to use it in the shared library, you have to open it first.

- **SVGO Compressor:** It lets you compress the SVGO assets at the time of exports. You don't need to select the keys or press anything SVGO does the work. It will show on the documents window after the compression work is done. You can temporarily disable the plugin if you want SVG assets uncompressed. You can disable it from the **Preferences > Plugins** and unchecking the SVGO compressor. You can get the original, uncompressed code by right-clicking on the layer and then copy the SVG code. You can change the setting according to your need by choosing the **Plugins > SVGO Compressor > About SVGO Compressor** and selecting the **Edit SVGO setting**.

Design   Collaborate   Apps   Resources ∨   Pricing

‹ Extensions / Plugins

Color Variables Migrator
by Sketch

Migrate your Layers and Styles to use the new Color Variables feature in Sketch 69.

v1.0.0
October 1, 2020
Requires Sketch 69 or newer.

Sketch 69 introduced Color Variables, a powerful new feature that allows you to reuse colors across your document while maintaining consistency and making updates easy.

When you open a document with pre-69 color swatches, Sketch converts them to Color Variables.

All Plugins

Automate Sketch

It makes sketch more useful. This has many plugins combined in one. It fits into an artboard with a margin. It included height and width to the parent artboard and set the margins. It lets you swap the height and width for all selected layers. It enables you to resize selected layers with the aspect ratio. It allows you to increase or decrease width/height for the selected layer. The value can be increased/reduced in the preferences. It lets you create a bound layer with a selected layer. It allows you split the layer. It enables you to ungroup a shape layer. It helps remove all the transform for the chosen group and shape layers, but it does not do any help in changing the appearance. You can unlock all layers. It lets you show all layers in the current page or selected group. It enables you to toggle select group content on the click option. It allows you to choose all layers, groups, shapes, bitmaps, and symbol instances. It sets all layers by matching the layer's name. It lets you select parent groups and all sibling layers. It enables you to work with the artboard layers which are outside the artboard bounds. You can also choose none. You can also paste layers into a selected artboard. It lets you replace the selected layer with the sketch layer on the clipboard. You can also change the position of the new layer relative to the old coating. You can copy/paste the position and size of the layer. It lets you remove the redundant nested groups. You can remove empty groups. You can ungroup all the groups on the artboard. It enables you to remove the hidden layers. It eliminates the transparency layers. It lets you rename the selected layer and use a custom template. You can find and replace a layer name. You can clear the layer name and also union layers in the artboard. You can convert layer to outline in the artboard. You can toggle mask or unmask for selected layers. It lets you create a link symbol layer from an artboard. You can use the midpoint to change two objects' positions. It enables you to tile objects with grids or without orientation. It lets you do the vertical or horizontal tilings of things. It allows you to do the vertical or horizontal tiling based on the layer list location.

You can distribute the select layers with the same width/height. You can arrange selected layers or artboards. You can change the selected layer of artboards. It lets you invest position in the layer list. You can use collapse all groups for collapsing. You can use a custom template to change the text of the selected layers. You can copy texts and paste them in alphabetical order. For all text layers, you can increase, decrease, or set horizontally. You can remove truncate text settings. You can add ellipses at the start, middle, or end of the text when the text is Overflow beyond the layer bound. It lets you combine selected layers into one layer. You can change the text layout. You can add spaces between Western and Chinese. It enables you to replace fonts. You can resize text layers. It lets you toggle the selected text layers auto and fixed. You can cancel the specified name of the text layer so that you can use the layer name that follows the content. It let you add direct export of selected layers. You can use export presets to create a slice of the layer. It enables you to set the name, layer order, and export option for the new slice layer. It clear all the slices. You can clear all exportable settings. It lets you divide slides. You can save and load export presets. You can copy layers, image files, and photos from iOS and then paste them as artboards. You can also paste them as Symbols. You can use a selection object to create a new artboard. You can use the group to create a new artboard. You can change the artboard to the group. For selected layers, you can choose the parent layers. You can quickly rename an artboard. You can move the selected artboard or symbol onto some other page. It lets you export all artboards as SVG/PNG.

AEIconizer
It helps in the automatic scaling of app icon artwork in all sizes needed for the devices such as iOS and macOS. You can select any layer after you are done with creating an icon on any square-sized artboard. You can also choose nothing if you have only that artboard on the page. You can generate all the needed sizes for macOS and iOS by running this Plugin. Plugins help to replace all the generated artboards any time it runs but never delete the original artboard.

Palette Cleanser helps you get down all the list of colors you are using in the sketch. You may download and install the latest version of it. You can build a palette by choosing plugins > Palette Cleanser > Build Palette. You can also press the ⇧⌘P on the keyboard to do the same. These will help in generating a Palette cleanser that appears on the first page of the sketch documents. You are advised not to change the artboard's name. Your current document gets separated into two columns, and the artboard shows all the colors. Palette cleanser will have layer-style colors and unique colors. Layer-style colors come from the fills and borders in the layers. It is straightforward to use and update them. They are the color that comes from a defined layer style in the document or a sketch library. You will find the following for each color:

- You will get a swatch of color.

- You will get the layer style name where the color appears.

- You will get the color hex value and opacity.

- You will get to know how many times color is used in the documents.

Unique colors come from the fills and borders in your document that are not part of the layer style. It works on simple design, but as the complexity of the designs increases, then it becomes difficult to use them. For each of these colors, you can find the following:

- You will get to know if any color is changed, added, or removed.

- You will get to know if any layer is shifted, added, or removed.

- You will get to know if any shared style is applied, created, or renamed.

You can always build back Palette cleanser if your document colors get out of sync. You can also remove the Palette by selecting the Remove Palette from the Palette cleanser in the plugins menu. You can also press the ⌥ + ⌘ + P. You can always give feedback on the GitHub.

Color Copy paste lets you copy/paste color directly from the phone's camera to design plugins.

Move to Library Sketch Plugin

You can move any symbol from your project to the library. You can also attach symbol instances to the library. It helps you keep the overrides without any problems. It also works with such abstracts which do not have libraries in local devices.

You can select one or more symbol instances and then select Move all Symbols to Library or Move selected Symbols to Library from the plugin menu. You can choose your library and put a check on it. It needs to be noted that you need to organize the library symbol names and symbols in your project. You can make the same component with the same name. You need to remove the duplicate name else, it creates complexity, and you may suffer. Plugin will take some time if your documents have too many symbols.

Crowdin Plugin for the Sketch

It helps you in connecting the sketch and the crowdin together. You can localize the UI and review the design within different languages before programming starts. It is elementary to send the whole page or separate artboard for translation to the crowdin. You can fetch the translation back to sketch. You can also preview and do the customization of translated copy directly in sketch. You can use the source strings from crowdin in your sketch project and upload artboard screenshots. You can use sketch runner to install the plugins. You can start working with the Plugin by following certain norms such as:

- You need to generate the personal access token in the crowdin account setting.

- You need to have an organization domain name.

- You need to link to the crowdin project.

The first two, access token and organization domain, are the global parameters used across all sketch projects. You need to define the crowdin project for each sketch project.

You can contribute to the sketch crowdin plugin by doing the following things:

- You need to fork the repository on GitHub.

- You need to decide which code you want to submit. You can then commit your changes accordingly and push to the new branch.

- You need to make sure that your code adheres to standard conventions as used in the rest of the library.

- You can also demand a pull request on your patch.

Sketch MeaXsure

It is re-implementation of the sketch measure. You can share the design specification, but there is a drawback, and that is the lack of maintenance. It is not likely to break down after the sketch update. It is easy to maintain and more stable. There are specific improvements that users can recognize:

- It works fully with sketch latest version sketch v66.

- It supports the newest Tint features.

- It does not concern breaking the marker but can easily resize them.

- There is an anima stack that lets you export directly.

- You can customize the order of the exported artboard.

- It allows you to display of text fragments.

- It enables you to recognize functions and panel.

If you face any problems and if you require any help, then you can run the menu as:

Plugin-Sketch MeaXure- Help – Rename Old Markers

Mesh Gradient

It lets you create an excellent mesh gradient inside the sketch. You can find all the mesh gradients at meshgradients.com. It has never been easy to create a mesh gradient. You need to set your mesh, pick some color, and then you can start making some curvy gradients. You can also use Collection gradient to bootstrap your new collection. You can use mesh gradient on any shape as a fill. The image fill created can be used on any layer, and you can also extend by playing with additional properties right in the Inspector panel. It can be used any image fill to adjust Fill, Fit, Tile, and stretch. You can also tweak the gradient as many times as you wish. You can safely store the gradient in the sketch file. This makes it easier to tweak any time when you need. You can create a 3D mesh by using the three.js, and it lets you Hermite the bicubic color interpolation to generate an excellent real mesh gradient. You don't need to play around with the circles and tons of blur. You can bootstrap your new collection by using a gradient from the selection.

Imgcook

It helps us to transform the design into code. It is light-weight and easy to use. It generates maintainable code, quickly visible, and intelligent identifiable. It uses advanced technology such as computer vision, in-depth learning, etc. They break the limitation of design drafts and help in generating intelligent code. It has one-click intelligent transformation and a robust operation panel. There is quality code that is derived from the design. It has multiple code templates and can be customized. The limitation to this is the ability of custom code is not open to everyone. It supports many code templates such as mini-app, Reacts, Weex, etc. It has high maintainability. It has an under-standable DOM structure, relative layout, and adaptive text. You can detect the link rendering very quickly, and the class selector is semantic. You can integrate this into the R&D process. It can download the generated code to any directory in just one click. The R&D link is connected to the support custom machining. You shall take care of a specific protocol. When there is a need to merge multiple layers into a single image, then the branch should select the relevant layer and merge them with one click. You can do two core operations, such as merging images and nodes into groups. It makes generated code absolutely accurate. You need to create a new artboard document to output the design. You can assume that imgcook is an ingenious chef who specializes in cooking with various images. It can sketch/PSD/still images. It generates maintainable UI view code by using a variety of visuals. It helps in improving the development efficiency of the front end. It lets the front-end engineers, designers and testers collaborate efficiently. The Alibaba front-end team, in fact, uses Imgcook. Tmall double eleven activity got improved, and the code availability went to 79% after generation.

Sketch Flat Export

You can export file symbol and layer into manageable file names. You can do this in one folder. You don't need to change the sketch symbol nesting and naming conventions. The sketch symbols contain icon/book, icon/calendar, icon/caret down, icon/caret right, icon/close, icon/close white, and icon/college. You can download the sketch plugin file and double click on it. You can choose a name format between the kebab_case, snake_case, or camel_case. It uses the full layer name while exporting. For example, the layer Icon/Search export as icon-search. svg, and then turn off, then it will be exported as search. svg. It is possible to add text to the beginning of the file name. For example, company-icon –search.vsg.you can export file format in the svg, png, or jpg.

Slint

It is a linter for sketch files. This is helpful in the case of shared libraries on which people collaborate. You can download and install it. The Find Dirty Styles: It helps us find the layers which are not in sync with the shared layers. You can choose the Plugins > Find Dirty Styles > Find Text Style.

Labelizer

It helps you extract all labels present in your sketch file. Then you can edit those labels in the table and can be exported to the page. Using this, you can easily translate a design. There is a particular set of critical values defined:

- Artboardname_Symbol_fieldname

- Artboardname_Symbol

- Artboardname_fieldname

- Artboardname_Sharedname

You can use JSON/CSV format to export/import the translation. The obvious idea behind the creation of this Plugin was to create a link between the creator, designer, and the developer. Everyone who is seeing the sketch file can easily understand the element stand for and the transition from one party to another. The Plugin navigates through each of the artboards present in the sketch. It should be noted that a proper name must be given to each element as that will act as an identifier for labels. The following elements are retrieved:

- Symbol

- Text

- Artboard

- Master symbol

The name preceded with [x] will be skipped during the extraction process. There is a specific list of common shared names:

- Tab.

- Title.

- Continue button.

- NextButton.

- back button.

- PreviousButton.

- CancelButton.

First, you need to download the zipped file and then extract it in a folder. The Plugin appears under the tab Plugin/LabelizNG/Labelize. After it is opened, it will be linked to the current file. You can link it to another by closing it. You can import a file that is exported by a plugin using the Plugin. There will be a table that will contain all the displayed files. You can modify from here and translate the page. You can also save your work by cling on Go to Download. The file is also made exportable there.

Check Contrast
It helps in getting the contrast ratio between the two layers with real-time feedback. You can view the color contrast ratio in the panel and also be able to pick colors at the same time. You can choose a layer and use a plugin to get the best background color for this. You can also check it for two

colors by just selecting both the colors and the Plugin will do the rest for you.

Cloudinary Plugin

It helps the developers fetch the images from the Cloudinary DAM. Using this, you can also upload artboard directly to Cloudinary using an upload reset. The images fetched will be optimized with the g_auto and q_auto. This Plugin was developed as part of the hackathon.

Symbol Insert

It is used to insert symbols in the sketch. You can download and install the latest version. It is generally helpful in handling the symbols from the shared libraries and local symbols. You can place a symbol with your mouse when inserting. There is support to partial text filter. You can open this through Plugin > Symbol Insert.

Flow Arrows

It lets you create user flow, sitemaps, and many more. You can choose two objects and then click on the Plugins > Connection arrows > Create Connection, which will create a connection. It automates the process, and you do not need to spend time on connecting and drawing arrows for user flows. You can create a connection as discussed. You can update all the connections inside the artboard. You can choose the artboards where all arrows are placed and then click on the Plugins > Connection arrows > Update Connection. You can also delete the connection by choosing Plugins > Connection arrows > Delete Connection > between selected. By default, it is an auto mode to draw an arrow in the direction of the second layer, but if you need to create user flow or sitemap, all arrows are pointed in one direction, and this can be set in the setting. You can also pre-define spacing between the arrows. That would automatically move the second layer for a specific amount of pixel when you create or update a connection between two objects. You can also choose the arrow style from the setting. You have straight, angled, or curved arrow types. They are saved globally and taken automatically according to the objects.

Live Planet Sketch Data Supplier
It was created using skpm. You can install the dependencies by:

```
npm install
```

It lets you run commands inside the projects:

```
npm run build
```

You can also watch the changes:

```
npm run watch
```

You can also run the plugin every time it builds:

```
npm run start
```

You get two options to customize the babel:
You can create a .babelrc file in your project's root directory. The setting written there will override the matching config keys within that skpm preset. Suppose you pass a

preset object, then it will reset all babel preset, and that skpm has by default. You can use webpack.skpm.config.js to modify or add existing babel config. You can customize the webpack by webpack.skpm.config.js file. Here is the function that mutates the original webpack config.

```
@param{object}
@param{boolean}
Module.export=function(config,
isPlugincommand)
{
}
```

You can view the output of the console.log by using the sketch-dev-tools. You can also open the console.app and look for the sketch app. You can look at ~Library//logs/com.boheamiancoding.sketch3/Plugin Output.log file.

You can do the latter using the skpm. If you use −f, then it causes skpm log not to stop when the end of records is reached. It will wait for the additional data to be appended. You can also publish your plugin.

Skpm publish <bump> where bump can patch, minor, or significant. The skmp publish will help create a GitHub repository, and to notify the sketch users, it makes an appcast file. You can specify the repository in package.json.

Persian Supplier

It supplies Persian data to sketch. It has the following features:

1. Name.

2. City.

3. Province.

4. Country.

5. Date.

6. Phone number.

7. Time.

8. Zip code.

9. Address.

10. Job.

You can reveal the plugin folder by choosing the Sketch App Menu > Plugins > Manage Plugins > Gear icons > Show Plugins Folder. You can delete the previously installed version of the plugin.

Chemfill

It fetches random molecules from ChEMBL API and returns a PNG image as rendering data. It is pretty is designing the structure of life sciences where the chemical structure might be a common form of data. You can access Chemfill from the sketch data menu once you have installed it. You can insert a random structure. The common inserting is molecular structure into a shape. You can select and right-click on the shape you would like to insert a chemical structure into. You can choose the data from the context menu. You can select a random structure. You can also insert random chemical data as text. This can be done by selecting the text box and right-clicking on it. Then you need to go to the Chemfill menu to choose the type of data you want to generate.

ASSISTANTS

It helps you check the inconsistencies or issues. They will check against a particular set of rules when you upload the documents. You can know which layer the issues relate to, and then you can fix that there itself. You can install and manage assistance in a straightforward way. There is no limit to add as much assistance as you wish to. Assistance might come for different reasons. Some might be there for the company's design system, some for the accessibility, and some for the document organization. The assistance stays attached to the Document even when you share them with others. They are added as per the basis of the documents. Another person with whom you shared the Document must have an assistant installed to see that else they will be prompted to install the assistant. You can use assistance to any other document other than the one on which you installed, and you just need to enable the assistant.

Working with the Assistant

They will check on the list of issues they have been conveyed to review as they are designed in that way. Assistant check against the inconsistencies, if any; they have specific built-up rules based on which they check. Assistance runs automatically, and when you make changes to the Document, they automatically update their results. You can also stop the assistant from running automatically. You can choose the **File > Assistant > Check Document Automatically**. You can toggle this option off from the menu bar. When you switch off the automatic checking, you need to enable checking by choosing the **File > Assistants > Check Document Now** or press the ⌘ + ⇧ + B for automatic checking. You can check this anytime to make the assistant update the result. You can check the Document and look at the errors after adding an assistant. The notification badge appears next to the assistant toolbar item. You can see the list of issues from there. You can fix a problem, and the assistant will check it. After that, it will disappear from the result list as you have set the case. You can choose the **View > Show/Hide Assistant** to show or hide the assistant result window at any time. Alternatively, you can also press ⌘ + ⌥ + 3. You can see the following in the result window:

1. The assistant will show the current number of issues which it has found. They have their thumbnail and notification badge. You can click on the thumbnail filter to show the problems from the selected assistants. You can view the issue from all assistants by using the leftmost thumbnail. It will reset the View.

2. You can access the Document Setting Window by using the circle icon. This is the link to show or hide rules, and you can open the assistant directory from here.

3. Will you get it? The icon when you hover over each issue in the result list. You can open the documentation for that specific rule by clicking on the list. The assistant's developer makes these.

4. Each issue shows specific layers. You can hover over the layer and find an → icon. You can go directly to that layer on the Canvas by clicking on this icon. You can also **reveal** to find it on Canvas by control-clicking on it.

You can ignore issues. Sometimes you may not find the notifications given by the assistant not helpful. The rules it is checking against might not be the necessity. You can ignore the message and issues on the specific layers. You can open the assistant result window to ignore the particular topics by clicking on that icon, and you can skip the issue by control-clicking on the layer which includes that issue. You can also choose to ignore in the contextual menu. You can control-click on the case described in the result window and decide to skip a problem for the entire Document. You can select the **Ignore rule for Document**. The result will be hidden from the list if you ignore the issue, either for the whole Document or a layer. You need to press on the three dots to view the complete result again. You shall select **Show Ignored issues**. The ignored issues will appear greyed out in the list. It happens after you set to show the ignore issues. The missed matters won't be counted in any badges, neither in the toolbar nor in the result window. You can set the result to show the ignored issue by stopping ignoring a problem in the result window. You can choose to **Stop Ignoring** from the contextual menu by control-clicking on the subject.

You can create assistants. There is an open platform where anyone can use JavaScript to build the assistant. The team can create their assistants. It will help them in the design system usage or style guide consistency. Here, an individual can share their best practices with others. You will find it very easy to build an assistant if you have prior experience making the plugin for Sketch. You still see the assistant more accessible even when you have not built the plugins before. You don't need to create UI in designing the assistant, whereas you need to make it while preparing the plugins. You just need to list down the rules for assistants to follow. You do not need every time to develop regulations; you can also adopt the ready-made rules and use them in your designs accordingly. You can go to developer docs to dive deep into the broader design community. You can also contact the developer team at developer@sketch.com.

Featured Assistants

5. **Sketch2React conventions:** It helps you with the sketch2React framework. It helps you in structuring documents. It lets you build responsive prototypes and very simple websites. You can use built-in tools inside the sketch app. You can head to Html or React when you are done with your masterpiece. The document must contain start here-@sketch2react-core-assistant/occurrence-of-page page. It must also contain the start here-@sketch2react/sketch2react-core-assistant/occurrence-of-artboard. It must contain a group name- @sketch2react/sketch2react-core-assistant-/group-name-component-name.

6. **Accessibility:** It assures the document is accessible with WCAG 2.1. It ensures that your sketch elements pass AA+ compliance based on web content accessibility guidelines. It is included as a feature in sketch 68. It detects accessibility infractions and sends the notification. It is not like the plugins. It has specific criteria to meets. It makes sure that shapes meet AA

color contrast compliance. It ensures that text must meet AA color contrast compliance. The text also meets AAA color contrast compliance. There are some issues with it, such as layers outside the artboards are not detected. It rarely sees the overlap of layers coordinates. To avoid false-negative, there is to be set 80% overlap rather than 1%.

7. **Organizer:** It keeps your documents neat and organized with the help of tips and suggestions. It will save the time you waste on organizing. The assistants spot the issues. Some of the drawbacks are there, such as abandoned layers, forgotten borders and fills, empty groups, and redundant styles. Following are certain assistant rules which you need to follow:

a. Group abandoned layers.

b. You need to remove the forgotten layers.

c. Remove the forgotten fills.

d. You can delete the empty groups.

e. It would be best if you ungrouped unnecessary groups.

f. You have to remove forgotten inner shadows.

g. Need to disregard shared style.

h. You need to follow naming conventions.

i. Remove forgotten shadows.

j. Respect text styles.

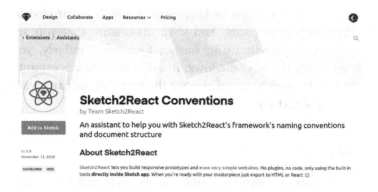

Sketch2React Conventions
by Team Sketch2React

An assistant to help you with Sketch2React's framework's naming conventions
and document structure

v1.0.9
November 13, 2020

GUIDELINES   WEB

About Sketch2React

Sketch2React lets you build responsive prototypes and even very simple websites. No plugins, no code, only using the built-in
tools **directly inside Sketch app**. When you're ready with your masterpiece just export to HTML or React ⤢

You can group the abandoned layer, which will make
your work organized and allow you to move things
together, reduce scrolling, and apply group properties. You
have already learned to create groups in detail in previous chapters. If you have a hidden border style, you can
remove such borders. You can add multiple borders with
different thicknesses, colors, and blend modes. You can
permanently remove what's not necessary. You can similarly remove the forgotten fills. Sketch provides you multiple fills types. It also lets you keep the layer clean and
neat. You can delete the empty groups which have no use.
Groups form an essential part of organizing things, using
tints features, and moving layers together. It would be best
if you ungrouped unnecessary groups as they are redundant. You have already learned in detail how to group and
ungroup. You can also remove forgotten inner shadows.
You can remove the unused ones and create multiple shadows. You can update and make a new shared style if the
shared styles are not working. You can follow the proper

naming conventions to keep your symbols organized in the component panel. You shall make sure that you are grouping symbols using slashes forward. Similarly, you can delete the new shadows. It will eliminate uncertainty in the designs. You can also set the text style or can create a unique text style.

All Assistants

8. **Tidy:** It helps your documents keep neat and clean. These are specific rules to be followed for using these assistants:

   k. It would be best if you did not disable borders.

   l. There shall be maximum ungrouped layers in the Artboard.

   m. You shall not disable the fills.

   n. You shall not disable the inner shadows.

   o. You shall not disable the shadows.

   p. Your layer style shall not be dirty.

   q. Your text style shall not be dirty.

   r. You shall not have empty groups.

   s. Your groups shall not be redundant.

   t. You shall not hide layers.

   u. Shared styles shall be used.

   v. Layers shall not be loose outside artboards.

9. **Reuse suggestions:** It gives you notice when it finds similar styles and groups which can be abstracted into shared styles and symbols. It has specific rules:

   w. It prefers the maximum number of identical layer styles to be 2.

   x. It prefers the maximum number of identical text styles to be 2.

   y. It prefers symbols and the maximum number of identical groups to be 2.

   z. It prefers color variables and the maximum number of identical colors to be 2.

10. **Naming conventions:** It is used significantly by the sketch design team. It has specific rules to be followed:

    aa. Page number shall start with emoji.

    bb. It demands that artboards' names shall start with numbers and be followed by spaces.

    cc. It has group forbidden.

    dd. There shall be used of a forward slash in the symbol name.

11. **Duplicate:** It reports various duplicate elements in your files. Duplicate files such as symbols, layer style, and text style are reported if duplicate. If it is inconsistent, redundant styles, then you get informed. It has rules for:

    ee. Duplicate layers style

    ff. Duplicate symbols

gg. Duplicate text style

hh. Duplicate artboard

12. **Stratos Token 2021 conventions:** It helps you with the 2021 conventions. It is a companion app for mac and pc that outputs design tokens and theming code.

13. **Mistica Linting:** It helps to keep your files full mistica.

14. **Neutral Guidelines assistance:** It observes the guidelines defined by the unbiased UX team. It has specific linting rules:

   ii. Opacity shall match the defined token values. If a font is found different than the JSON file, then it shall report a violation.

   jj. It shall match the defined radius values, and if any violation happens then, it reports it.

   kk. Shadows shall match the value defined of the JSON file, and it reports violations if made any.

   ll. Border style shall match as in the JSON file, and if there is any violation, then it will report it.

   mm. Border color shall match as defined in the JSON files, and if there is any violation, then it will report it.

   nn. Similarly, fills color shall match as defined in the JSON files, and if there is any violation, then it will be reported.

   oo. Text color shall match the defined standard in JSON files, and if there is any violation, then it will report.

pp. Text size shall also meet the token values defined in the JSON files, and if there is any violation, it will be reported.

qq. Text line height shall meet the defined token values in the JSON files, and if there is any violation, it will be reported.

rr. Text font family shall meet the token values in the JSON files, and violations, if any, will be reported.

ss. Similarly, artboard names shall meet the token values defined in the JSON file, and violations will be reported if made any.

tt. Symbol name shall follow the value defined in the JSON files, and a violation will be reported if made any.

uu. Text content shall also meet the value defined in the JSON file.

15. **Lightning Design System Linter:** It is an assistant for salesforce lightning design system. It validates documents, text colors, fill colors, and border colors, and it helps in adjusting the salesforce lightning design system. You shall make sure that you are using the correct SLDS version. There are specific rules for using Linter. You shall make sure that fill colors shall match the SLDS background or generic color token. You shall make sure that the border color matches the SLDS border. You shall also confirm that text color matches the generic color token values. Text size shall match the SLDS font size.

16. **Documents Stats and Coverage:** It helps you check the coverage levels and components used across the documents. You can get the stats by enabling the free flow DS assistants. You will get the following information about your file:

vv. You will get the Text Layer Coverage.

ww. You will get the Layer style Coverage.

xx. You will also get the symbol usage counts.

yy. You will get the detached symbol counts.

zz. You shall make sure that you are using Sketch 68 or the above version. You can install the free flow document stats and coverage assistant.

INTEGRATIONS

You can integrate apps with Sketch and make the work more interesting.

Featured Integrations

1. **Lokalise:** You can download the lokalise plugin as a zip file and open the lokalise.sketchplugin. You can exchange text and translation between Sketch and lokalise. You will get the corresponding translation of the desired language and be inserted into proper text elements. It lets you push text to lokalise. You can pull translated text from lokalise. It enables you to set the key name. It allows you to set a character limit for created keys. You can create new keys or match text

to existing keys. You can seamlessly switch design language.

2. **Maze:** You can test your prototypes with the Maze. It will provide you valuable insights. You can do one click from the prototype URL and bring a sketch mockup to the Maze. It speeds up the product iteration and makes a better and faster user experience. You can share the maze result with dynamic charts, call-out quotes, unique usability scores, and empowering collaboration.

3. **Flinto:** It is used by the developer to create interactive design and animated prototypes. You can use the free trial. It works on macOS 10.14 and iOS 12.0 or newer. You can design transitions between the screen. You can navigate the prototype using the tap, swipe, scroll, and even 3D touch. You can preview your work in real time. You can add haptics feedback that users can is experienced on the iOS device. It lets you create animation using 3D tools. You can design UI right inside the flint with an advanced vector drawing tool. You can create scroll-based animations. You can attach an audio file for UI sound effects. You can record a prototype to share it online. You can also import your design from Sketch or Figma. It has 100+ tutorial videos, an extensive documentation. It provides you fine-tuned control over cubic-bezier or spring easing for every layer. You can drag video or GIF files directly into your designs. You can send your recording directly to the Dribble.

All Integrations

17. **Abstract:** It has a design workflow management system, and it let the design member and stakeholder to manage and collaborate on the Sketch. It gives your team spaces for communication. It has more tools and dependencies that can automate the work. No one considers the business impact of decision-making. It has an intelligent design platform. You can prioritize your design work and collaborate with the rest of the people to view their work. You can review their work and make a better design or product. It lets you collaborate without overwriting each other's work. You can read the report of about 1000 people designer work and what they value.

18. **Avocode:** It lets you to inspect Sketch documents, and you can quickly get access to the CSS fonts, image assets, dimensions, and colors. It let you turn the design into code. You have the option to get the handoff, Inspect, Get Assets, and Review. You can ship apps and pixel-perfect websites at two times speed. You can import any design format such as Figma, Sketch, photoshop, and Adobe XD. It lets you generate and customize code snippets, export assets, and measure sizes. The app works fine on macOS, Windows, and Linux. It let you switch between CSS, Swift, XML, and React Native. It enables you to customize the code output, reorder its properties, and hide it. You can use the proper resolution to export all assets. You can export the design in PNG, JPEG, SVG, and WEBP. It lets you set a custom export scale and

path. You can get the dimensions of any layer and its distances from other layers. You can get these values in px, pt, or percentages. You can visually compare the style by placing the design on top of the coded layout. You can also note the difference and matches in the style. It helps us save a considerable amount of time. There are both web apps and desktop app.

19. **Crystal:** It lets you preview your Sketch designs in real time. You can preview it on android devices. You can use this to preview and prototype sketch design. It is relied on by google, Apple, and Expedia. You can preview your design in real time by opening the Crystal on the same WiFi as your computer. When you modify your Artboard in Sketch, then Crystal refreshes on the fly. You can also use a USB when you don't have WiFi or in a corporate network. You can move screens by swiping between adjacent Artboards or Prototypes. It fully supports Sketch Prototyping, including the transition animation and android back button navigation. You can also preview the mobile app design on the devices they are made for. It automatically matches the pixel Artboard, so compatible with screen fit. You can view the entire screen on tablets. You can save the document for offline access. You can access it without Sketch. You can do the complete prototyping offline. The Crystal app runs with the companionship of Sketch. Crystal version v3.4.0 will let you fix high-quality rendering. It has easier Artboard control. Version 3.5.0 allows your computer to auto-connect with the Crystal. This version has hard to find Artboard. It will let you try the searching.

Version 3.5.3 will let you use sketch cloud support. It has a bit of bright orange Artboards. Version v3.5.5 has a clever interface to display the fixed layers. V3.6.0 allows us to maintain the scroll position in the prototypes. It occupies only 3.4M space. V3.6.2 is the latest version to use. You can get interactive elements on purchase. It requires an Android 5.0 or up version. It is offered by smithy productions.

20. **Draft:** It has simple sidebar navigation and helps showcase your design. It lets access to every screen by URL address. It is the perfect tool to share and store the web and interface design screen. It stores the screen in perfect order. You can organize and structure the screen. It has a site-tree view that keeps the state and resolutions together. You can share your project design by copying the link address. It has no distractions and zero UI with a precise retina scale. It has a good intuitive drag and drop interface. You can use the open graph to direct link sharing. It has a collaborative approach. It has no interface preview mode. It has an activity waterfall. It lets you upload the design from the Sketch. It enables you to comment. You can have one-click access to the entire project in the Draft. It allows you to stay up to date. You have an activity overview where you can follow the team members' updates and uploads across all projects. You can upload the design directly from Sketch. It lets you exports artboards directly from Figma. You can have a quick and focused presentation. You can check the appearance of the project when they are made public in Draft.

21. **Droplr:** It lets you upload artboards directly to Droplr. You can share and get valuable feedback from there. It enables you to Collaborate with others without hassle. You can share artboards. You can use the communication channel to share your work with anyone. It lets you speed up the projects. Your client will find it very easy to share their valuable feedback. You can also collaborate with nontech users and avoid tech overload. It lets you capture screenshots and screen recording instantly. You can share the link of the document, which is saved to the cloud. It is available for mac, Windows, Chrome, and Chromebook. You can also annotate by adding the text in the screenshots. It has an optional webcam as GIF or HD video. You can take partial or entire screen recordings. It has unlimited GIF recording duration. Your screen recordings and screenshots are saved to the cloud, and you will have the link to it on the clipboard. You can share it with anyone anywhere by just copy/pasting the link and sharing it with others. You can also download it as PNG or WebM. You will have your personal droplr account where these recordings and screenshots are located. It lets you eliminate the clutter of the screenshots and screen recording. It has a file uploader and link shortener. You can upload your files in the cloud. You can share up to 10GB files by just the drag and drop method. You can shorten the link by using a URL shortener. You can also view analytics. Droplr integrates with Google Docs, Gmail, Sketch, and many more.

22. **Flow:** It lets you create excellent UI animations. It lets you import, animate, and export sketch design to production-ready code the developers use. It does not require any code. It allows seamless transmission from Sketch, Figma, and SVG to flow in seconds. It has no learning curve, but it has a robust, intuitive motion design. You can use the production-ready code from there. You can import from Sketch, Figma, and SVG effortlessly. You will have all the properties of the shapes, text, and images to animate. You can embed them easily in your web flow site. It lets you use customizable code exports. You can use layers and properties to create complex animations and interactive elements. It provides you an intuitive path editing interface and a custom curve editor. It has 1/100s precision. With a simple push, you can export your saved animations to Swift, Lottie, web, animated SVGs, and React. It lets you animate the shapes, images, and text.

23. **Framer:** It is one of the powerful prototyping tools for mac users. It lets users create, invent and experiment with the animations and interactions in CoffeeScript. It is a one-time tool. It enables the Framer to help the team in designing every part of the product experience. You do not require any code to start in Framer and get a functional output. You can unlock more interactivity. Framer provides first-class interaction throughout the whole workflow, such as wireframing, visual design, design system, handoff, prototyping, and user testing. You can use transition, animations, and intelligent components to create prototypes in Canvas. It provides you better feedback from the user

test, applicable handoff code for engineers. You can use Framer to design anything. You can get interactive designs in a minute with intelligent features, layout tools, drag and drop components and building blocks, and many more. You get collaboration as a loop and not as a cycle. There is also asynchronous collaboration in the design tool. Framers help you deep-dive into detailed collaboration, and it lets designers to work in more profound ways in the team. It enables designers to plug into existing workflows used by UX researchers, developers, and copywriters. You can try the accessible version of the Framer.

24. **Frontify:** It is a brand management tool that connects the design team members with stakeholders such as marketing and brand. You can find all brand assets available in Sketch, and it also pushed back designers for handover. It has centralized repositories, which help in connecting the design teams. You can manage Frontify based design files, and it can be done in Sketch directly. It lets you access the brand assets directly within the Sketch. You can also simplify the design production. You can use brand elements living in Frontify, such as colors and typographies, and you can also implement them. It lets you keep track of best practices and design documentation. It enables you to upload an artboard created in the Sketch to Frontify. From there, you can know the approval, feedback, and documentation. It lets you sync the specs living in the Frontify with the Sketch. It will keep the designer forever on brand. You can access documented brand colors, fonts in the Sketch. You can access assets such

as icons, logos, and images from fortify in the Sketch. It has an active sketch account. You will get creative collaboration as a part of the Frontify plan.

25. **Envision:** It helps the designers with the prototyping, collaboration, and presentation. It is the best-known platform for the designers. You can take a design from ideas to development in one forum. You can collaborate in real time to using an endless digital whiteboard. You can start with a pre-built template or blank Canvas. You can create a rich, interactive prototype. You can also import anything from Sketch and collaborate with others. It lets to involve developers. You can collect inputs and provide detailed specs to keep builds on the track. It has some essential integration in which you can connect your workflow. You can streamline your entire product by using existing tools in InVision. It helps in bringing all the components, codes, and principles into one centralized place. It has sync, which changes globally through the Sketch. You can connect design to code with the storybook. It acts as a single source for design, product, and development. It has a stunning screen design that amplifies your creative expression. You may request a demo at their official site.

26. **Kite Composer:** It is one of the powerful animation and prototyping applications for Mac and iOS. You can use the trial version or buy at their official website. It is usually called as after effect of the Sketch. You can build a complex interface by the visually drag and drop method. You can add animations and tune them with an integrated timeline. It is just

like paint code for core animation. It uses the built-in JavaScript scripting environment to enhance the detail of each interaction. You can achieve exactly what you need by incorporating the custom logic and behavior. There is a new update available for macOS 10.15 Catalina. You can explore the example from the documentation part. It has amazing tools and features to help bring the user interface to life. You can drag and edit animation durations and keyframes using an innovative integrated timeline. You can get a precise hand-tuned feel by snapping animation start and end times. You can edit all of the layers in a few clicks using a robust and powerful object inspector. It lets you set colors, adds core images, adjusts animation curves. You can build your interface visually by dragging and dropping the layers from the library. You can also save reusable layers in the hierarchies. It lets you use it easily. You can download the native companion app for an iOS device like kite Compositor for iOS. You can also generate native animation code. It lets you generate zero dependencies, swift, or objective-C code for the animation. You can generate code compatible with both Mac and iOS. It frees you from guessing how large it shall grow, how fast something should move, and how to ease between keyframes. It works with adobe XD CC. you can design your workflow in adobe XD CC and then import it to the kite for final animation. You can also preserve animation properties such as Bezier paths, colors, text attributes, and shadows. You can move a movie or GIF to share your design. You can use the kite native import feature to import designs from the Sketch easily. You can preserve the Bezier paths and text. You can do so by importing your Sketch layers as native kite layers. You can add sophisticated logic to your animations and interactions. You can use a built-in JavaScript scripting engine. You can use a built-in JavaScript console to make live edits to your running animations. You can add new layers and fire animations. You can download the kitekit framework and play. kite documents within the iOS and Mac apps. You can design, embed, and play. It was built by using macOS native core animation technology. It is one of the underpinning graphic technology and provides stunning animations at high framerates.

27. **Lingo:** It is used as a design system manager in the Sketch. You can set up, use, and evolve a shared design system. You can organize all the visual assets in one place using the Lingo app. It lets you create and share the living brand style, digital assets, libraries, and more. It enables you flexible ways to organize assets. It would be best to design according to your requirement partly Lingo is brand style guides and partially digital assets management. You can bring the context and content to a single place. You can share your visual assets with the team or the public. You have three options; private, password-protected, and public. You can control the privacy of brand visual assets. It ensures consistency and empowers teams. It has powerful image processing capabilities such as repetitive tasks like file conversion and resizing. You can create and share in your own way. You can use a

single tool to build different types of assets libraries. This way, all the visual assets are made and stored at a single location. It will help in productivity and brand consistencies. The files in hides in a folder that lives in Lingo. You can create a living brand style guides. You can use a visual hub for Figma and sketch assets. You can also build a digital assets library. Earlier, Lingo finding assets was to mean it dig manually through the drivers, servers, and folders. Now, it is possible to locate design and illustrations visually.

28. **Marvel:** It can turn your web sketches, images, and mock-ups into mobile and web prototypes. It lets you do rapid prototyping, testing, and handoff for the new modern design teams. It changes the perception about creating the digital products. Now, the power of design is in everyone's hands. It keeps your intuitive designs and prototype in one place. It can be a wireframe, design, and prototype. It can power up the workflow by generating the design specs and connect integrations. You can create beautiful interfaces and wireframes. You do not require any code to make the design interactive. It has a mechanical design for development. It has centralized feedback and ideas. The world's most innovative companies use it to scale innovation. There are many digital products that you might have used that are made by the Marvel. It is used by start-ups, fortune 100, to school children. You can collaborate and optimize prototypes before development. It is built to take care of the needs of the large teams. Marvel 3 is constructed primarily with fast technology and makes the design more interactive.

CONCLUSION

In this chapter, we learned about Sketch Extensions. We learned about different Plugins. We understood the working of the assistant and how they help in Sketch. We understood the Integrations in Sketch.

Appraisal

When it comes to prototyping and designing for the web in real time, nothing beats Sketch. Even though it is still a primarily mac app, Sketch has found many loyal users even since its inception.

This book covered in brief all the salient aspects of designing in Sketch. Here is a rundown of what we learned:

One of the exciting features of the Sketch **Canvas** is that you can navigate around it. There are a bunch of zoom options available to explore in Canvas. You can see the pixels, pixels grid, and rulers. It is pretty easy to measure the distance between two layers.

The **Inspector** in the Sketch lets you work with the borders such as inside border and outside border. You can also preview and export an Artboard. You can work with blurs such as usual blur and background blur. You can see the canvas area by enabling the rulers. You can define Grid block size and thickness. Columns are usually used to align things.

You can switch between components view and canvas view. The **customization** of the toolbar in the Sketch is also an exciting feature. The Layer list contains all Artboard, pages, and layers. It is handy to use pages while working with complex documents. The **Artboard** plays a significant role in the design of screen size. Although they are optional features,

DOI: 10.1201/9781003261575-9

they find elementary uses in sketches. It is pretty interesting to resize an Artboard and move Artboard. It is fun working with the Layer Style, Text Styles, and Color Variables. You can use the toolbar between other components.

The contextual menu lets you create, rename, and copy CSS attributes. You can make changes to a specific Text Layer and all Text Layers at the same time. You can use the Component View panel to insert Text with Style. It lets you perform various operations such as update, create, and detach. **The Layer Style** works with the Shapes instead of Text, as in the case of Text Style. You can insert text or layer style via insert window and component view. **The Color Variable** has sync features that make changes appear everywhere. There are existing global color presets which are part of color variables in the library. There are two methods similar to text and layer style in the color variable to add the color variable. The component view plays an essential role in adding the color variables. The Inspector and Find and Replace menus are equally important. Editing color variables is one of the best parts of the Sketch. There are many other operations you can perform in color variables, such as rename, delete, find, and replace color variables. The Inspector has significant uses in resizing constraints and layer properties.

Shapes are a different topic of interest in Sketch. You can adjust shapes dimensions such as radius, width, and height. You can edit Shapes in Vector Editing mode.

Working with **Layers** is relatively easy. You can add Layers, select them, and group them. You can also select the overlapping layers. You can make Grids in Sketch. You can define Grids dimensions. There are different types of **alignment**, such as left, right, horizontal, vertical, and center of layers. **Smart distribution** is a unique feature for the same purpose. Inspector lets you resize the layers. You can perform various operations on layers such as rotate, duplicate, and select layers.

Sketch also lets you **style** the Layers. You can define **Presets** and **Gradients** in Sketch. **Tints** allow you to apply a specific color to the whole group or symbol. You can set as many borders as you can in layers. It enables you to adjust the position of the border. You can use **Shadows** and **Inner Shadows** for rendering outside and inside the layer. There are multiple types of blurs available such as **Gaussian blurs, motion blurs, zoom blur, and background blur**. Similar to layer style, there is text style, but here, you work with the Text instead of shapes. You can perform all the operations such as organizing, grouping, etc.

Vector Editing in Sketch lets you draw and edit Shapes. You do various operations with the points, such as select, move, change point types, insert a point, and bend a segment. You can open and close the path connecting two points. It lets you turn a border into an outline. You can reverse the order of the path. You can add premade shapes, use pencil tools, and edit shapes in the Inspector. You can use the Transform tool to edit shapes. Sketch lets you use **Boolean Operations**. You can **Mask** a shape. Sketch allows you to create and share a **Library**.

Sketch lets you work with the **Images and Data**. You can insert images, replace images, reduce image size, and edit bitmap images. There are different image fill types such as angular gradient, solid fill, linear-gradient, etc. There are **Color Popover** features that let you do various operations with the file icon, Text field, color picker, and Slider. **Data**

tool lets you add different Text and images to the documents. It helps you in creating realistic prototypes. You can use the Data tool on text data, image data, and linked data. Working with data provides you with data tab preferences. You can toggle visibility, add data, control-click, and use the menu. You need **JSON** files to work on Linked Data. You can add or insert **Text** and perform various other functions when you go to the text menu bar. Similarly, you can work with the **Symbols**. Any changes made to the symbols appear everywhere in the Sketch. You can insert a symbol through the insert window. You can edit a symbol in the Sketch and also detach the symbol if needed.

Sketch provides you intuitive **Prototyping**. It gives you hands-on experience in prototyping features. You can create **links** between Artboards. You can also decide the appearance of the link transition. You can add **hotspots** in prototypes. You can create a fixed layer position while scrolling in the menu. You can also maintain the scroll position after the click, which is discussed in Chapter 6 in detail. It lets you preview and share prototypes. It also enables you **Import/Export** the sketch files using the cloud or locally saved sketch documents.

Sketch lets you **Collaborate in Real-Time**. You can see the changes that others are making to the documents. You can also edit and save a new copy of the changes made by you. You can invite designers to collaborate on your projects. You can work and edit in real time.

There are **Extensions** available in a sketch which makes the prototypes more interactive and intuitive. You have **Plugins, Assistants, and Integration**, which add more life to your design and prototypes.

Index